WORDS AT WAR : WORDS AT PEACE

WORDS AT WAR
WORDS AT PEACE

*Essays on Language in General
and Particular Words*

by

ERIC PARTRIDGE

LONDON
FREDERICK MULLER LTD.
29 GREAT JAMES STREET, W.C.1

FIRST PUBLISHED BY FREDERICK MULLER LTD.
IN 1948
PRINTED IN GREAT BRITAIN
BY BUTLER & TANNER LTD.
FROME & LONDON

FOR
NEIL BELL

FOREWORD

THESE essays have, with one exception, been written during the period since 1938. Several have not hitherto been published ; I deliberately held them back for this collection, less of a hotch-potch than an unsympathetic critic might suppose.

Thanks are due—and hereby given—to the editors of the following periodicals for permission to reprint : *The Quarterly Review* (especially), *Chambers's Journal*, *The New Statesman and Nation*, *John o' London's Weekly*, *The Radio Times* and *The Jewish Outlook*.

CONTENTS

Part One : AT PEACE AND WAR

Part Two : SLANG

CONTENTS

Part One: AT PEACE AND WAR

Gatherations

A FEW years ago, *Punch* ran a series of three articles on Group Terms, otherwise known as Company Nouns or, by the learned, Terms of Assemblage. And in May 1939, Major C. E. Hare, in his invaluable book, *The Language of Sport*, gave a long list.

Originally, Company Nouns were connected with field sports, animals, birds, fishes ; so, still, are most of those Company Nouns which have survived ; an astonishing number of them have survived for nearly five centuries, as a glance at Dame Juliana Barnes's *The Book of St Albans*, 1486, will show. Even there, however, we find a few quite general terms, unconnected with field sports and the creatures that were hunted. Some technical Company Nouns have become general currency ; for instance, a *flock* of sheep, a *herd* of cattle (Australians prefer *mob*—a word they apply in many incongruous ways), and a *pack* of hounds. But some delightful general Company Nouns have fallen into disuse ; for instance, a *blush* of boys, a *boast* of soldiers, a *gaggle* of gossips, a *hastiness* of cooks, a *skulk* of thieves. This is a sad loss.

Certain moderns, however, have attempted to introduce Group Terms : with a courage and an ingenuity that have deserved a better fortune than they have experienced. Here are a few delights purveyed to us by *Punch*. A *guzzle* of aldermen ; a *boodle* of company promoters ; a *stodge* of Conservatives and a *heckle* of Socialists ; a *frolic* of 'flappers' ; a *slink* of mannequins ; a *flutter* of spinsters ; a *fleece* of punters ; a *gush* of poets. Colonel R. J. Nicol, in

3

A Collection of Terms, *denoting Assemblages*, 1933 (privately printed), coined the following felicities : a *condescension* of actors, a *giggle* of chorus-girls, a *blather* of generals (military, not domestic), a *futility* of husbands (as though they weren't sufficiently worried already !), a *muddle* of mayors. Soldiers appear to excel at this sort of thing, for to Lt-Colonel C. Bartley-Dennis we owe ' an *emulsion* of doctors ', ' an *unhappiness* of husbands ' (well, well !), and the supreme appositeness of a ' *click* of chorus-girls '. Major Hare has increased the gaiety of nations by his contribution of the following ' assemblages ' : a *surge* of book-makers and a *riot* of boys ; a *saunter* of loafers ; a *charm* of fairies ; a *trace* of virgins, the Major being a trenchant satirist as well as a potential poet.

After the perfection of ' a *click* of chorus-girls ', ' a *charm* of fairies ', ' a *frolic* of flappers ', it may seem to be an impertinence in me to append a short list of my own. But never let it be said that I'm not game—to be shot at (and, perchance, brought down) by the hunters.

Nationalities supply such Group Terms as the following :

A *guess* of Americans
A *courage* of Dutchmen
An *insularity* of Englishmen
A *dash* of Frenchmen
A *momentum* of Germans
A *brogue* of Irishmen
An *adaptation* of Japanese
A *gloom* of Russians
A *generosity* of Scotchmen
A *delight* of Turks
An *eisteddfod* of Welshmen

4

Society with a big and a little *s* is a very wide field ; a few gleanings will suffice.

A *dampness* of babies
A *scamper* of children
A *clutter* or a *jazz* of dancers
A *diffidence* of debutantes
An *overdraft* of fathers
A *daddy* of ' gold-diggers '
A *duster* of housewives
An *anxiety* of spinsters
A *rapacity* of ' sweet young things '
A *quo vadis ?* of wives
A *superiority* of young people

Now for the world's workers :

An *accent* of announcers (radio)
A *vanity* of authors
A *celerity* of aviators
A *bald spot* of barbers
A *burning* of cooks
A *drill* or *removal* of dentists
A *rejection* of newspaper editors
A *corner* of financiers
An *Ali Baba* of garage proprietors
A *growth* of gardeners
A *column* of journalists
A *surplus* of lawyers
An *undulation* of mannequins
A *neckerchief* of navvies
A *procrastination* of plumbers
A *pot* of publicans
An *expectation* of publishers
A *protection* of racketeers

A *collation* of scholars
A *quantum* of scientists
A *margin* of stockbrokers
A *see-saw* of surgeons
An *apology* of telephone operators

And a few odds-and-ends, just to give an air of comprehensiveness to an admittedly nondescript list :

An *elongation* of anglers
A *pavilion* of cricketers
A *highfalutin* of highbrows
An *earthiness* of lowbrows
A *proximity* of misers
A *licence* of motorists
A *hail* of Nazis
A *propaganda* of pacifists
A *morgue* of pedestrians
A *prosiness* of poets
A *serenity* of saints
A *pact* of statesmen

In the coining of Company Nouns, alliteration is occasionally helpful ; but far more important than alliteration is appositeness or point—or both. Whether directly or indirectly, one aims at a characteristic, above all at a failing, of the class or group that is to be named. One may be allusive, as in ' an *honour* of thieves ', or frankly condemnatory, as in ' a *tardiness* of taxi-drivers ', or even (apparently) inaccurate, as in ' a *caste* of playwrights '. One may, in short, be this, that, or the other : but never dull ; never stupid.

(An elaboration of my 1939 Christmas card.)

Note. A long article on this subject is included in *Usage and Abusage : A Guide to Good English.*

The New Year

IN ancient times, the commonest dates for the beginning of the year were September 21, December 21 and June 21 : such is the tyranny of the seasons, these being respectively the autumn equinox, the winter solstice and the summer solstice. The modern custom of holding New Year's Day on January 1 was introduced by Julius Caesar, but medieval Europe began the year on March 25, the official—though not, of course, the actual—spring equinox. It was not till early in the 18th century that Europe finally decided on January 1 ; and England, behind as usual, waited till the year 1750.

New Year as a festival of great jollity comes down to us from our Norse and Danish ancestors. The habit has continued. Scotland and the Continent still observe New Year's Day far more than Christmas Day, and, there, gifts are presented on January 1 ; they have tradition on their side, for the ancient Persians used to celebrate the day by exchanging presents of eggs ; in Rome the New Year gift was a regular institution, though, later, Tiberius forbade the giving or the receiving of such gifts ; the Druids solved the problem of ' what shall I give ' by distributing pieces of mistletoe, their sacred plant. In medieval England, and indeed until much later, the New Year gifts were one of the heaviest expenses chargeable to the King's purse : the modern counterpart is the New Year's List of Honours.

Apparently the actual words *New Year* were first written about 1200 A.D., though undoubtedly they were spoken

centuries before : ' Thatt dajj is New Jeress dajj mang
Enggletheode nemmnedd ', which being interpreted
meaneth : ' That day is New Year's Day as many English
people called it '. *New Year's tide*, much less heard now
than *Christmastide*, came into written use when Queen
Elizabeth mounted the throne.

Under the Stuart kings, especially after the Restor-
ation, there was a spate of poems, anonymous for the
most part, bearing some such title as *A New Year's Gift* ;
one of them was a hymn of hate flung at the political
enemies of England and her King.

But the strangest of all printed ' gifts for the New Year '
is the following poem, which presents a very pretty little
problem for the Sherlock Holmeses of literature to solve.
It is to be found buried at the British Museum in a volume
of debris enriched here and there with the ore of a Byron
or a Milman. Written, I suspect, by a disillusioned *Emigré*,
it is a tiny pamphlet of 16 pages, printed by one J. F.
Dove, of St John's Square, London, probably in the year
1816. Bearing the double title *New Year's Gift* and
Etrennes mignonnes (' dear little presents '), this anonymous
poem of seven stanzas, with the French on the opposite
page, purports to be the will of the great Napoleon. If the
French and the English are by the same person, then he
was enviably bi-lingual. The style is formal.

> The Emperor,
> Exil'd from France to St Helena's hell,
> Where none but devils can with pleasure dwell,

begins with Europe, to which, ' for its pains ', he leaves

> The conscious slavery of galling chains ;
> And next we freely give to wretched France
> The sad regrets of its Carmagnol dance,

an allusion to the French Revolution. There is, you see, something of the irony of Villon's famous *Last Will and Testament*. The author hits out at everybody :

> To all our relatives of high degree,
> We leave the spoils of pillag'd Germany ;
> Whose sons, in drinking never known to flag,
> In faith and in the field of battle lag.

To Talleyrand he bequeathes ' the sieve of Satan ' ; to Italy ' the fee simple of its ignominy ' ; to Spain and the Spanish, where he ' ne'er could reign ', nothing but ' the curses of their own chicane ' ; Switzerland is lashed for her ' degenerate aid ', Holland is vilified as ' a race of pedlars ', Austria called ' faithless ', the Pope mocked. He ends with his fiercest curse :

> To all, where fire and famine I've bestow'd,
> I leave my revolutionary code ;
> To England and its shop-bedizen'd trade,
> Of knights and knighthood all the dull parade.

(Written in 1938.)

9

Nicknames for Jews

'THERE are a good many traces in language of Christian brutality towards the Jew,' remarks Professor Ernest Weekley in the essay on ' Xenophobia ' in a fascinating book, *Words and Names*. The phrase *worth a Jew's eye* (extremely valuable) would seem to refer to eyes put out by medieval torturers to enforce payment. ' In the Middle Ages ', Weekley continues, ' all sorts of midnight iniquities and unholy rites were attributed to the Jew, with the result that the word *sabbat* acquired in French the sense of a sorcerers' nocturnal gathering. . . . This may possibly account for the *Jew's harp*, earlier also *Jew's trump*, which . . . was a favourite instrument at the " witches sabbath ". . . . One of the latest examples '—this book was published in the year preceding Hitler's accession to power—' of racial bad manners is the nickname *yid* for a Jew, [either short for *Yiddisher* or] a back formation from *yiddish* (German *jüdisch*), the *lingua franca* of the Israelites, made up from various sources but written in the Hebrew character.'

The basis of Yiddish is popular German, with admixtures from Hebrew, Russian, and other European languages. A speaker thereof is naturally a *Yiddisher*, from which derive the English *Yid* and the American *Yiddie* or *Yiddle* : these are among the commonest of all the nicknames for a Jew.

But before we pass to nicknames bestowed by Christians, we may note a particularly interesting one that is Jewish. The Sephardic Jews (the *Sephardim*), of Spanish or Portuguese descent, owe their name to the fact that they came from *Sepharad*, credibly identified with Spain ; by the non-Sephardic Jews (known as the *Ashkenazim*, the Ashkenazic Jews) the Sephardim are often called the *Gauchos*, with a neat double reference—to the Spanish *caballeros* (knights ; literally, horsemen) and to the Gauchos, those cowboys of the pampas who, notable horsemen, are of mixed Spanish and Indian descent. The word *Gaucho* probably comes from *cauchu*, ' wanderer '—in the language of the Araucanians (Indians of Central South America).

The racial names *Jew, Hebrew, Israelite,* have themselves been debased into such nicknames as *Jew boy* (English) and *Joosh*—or the *Chusen-pipples* (American), with obvious reference to *Jewish, Chosen people* ; *Hebe* and *Heebie,* used more in America than in Britain ; *son of Israel* and *Izzy,* likewise more American than British. Very American, too, is *House of David boy.* German-Jewish refugees are, in the United States, called *refujews.* Of the originating terms, by the way, *Jew* is that which is preferred by most of the self-respecting Christian writers, who leave *Hebrew* and *Israelite* to the more careless among the journalists ; *Jew* possesses a simple dignity lacking in its synonyms.

Given names—to avoid the ambiguity of the term *Christian names* and the invidiousness of *font names*—have generated a number of nicknames, such as *Abe* or *Abie* from ' Abraham ', *Ike* and *Ikey* from ' Isaac ' and *Ikey Mo* from ' Isaac Moses ', *Jake* from ' Jacob ', *Levi* from itself, and *Max.* Whereas *Ike* and *Ikey* (*Mo*) are typically British, the others are much commoner in the United States and, derivatively, Canada than they are in Britain. A Jewess is often called *Rachel* or *Rebecca*, from two of the most popular of all Jewish female names ; in America, she is often called a *kosher cutie, cutie* being ' a girl ', especi-

11

ally ' one's favourite girl ' or ' an attractive girl ' (she's so ' cute ' !), and originally a term employed by gangsters and racketeers, crooks and criminals, but now quite respectable.

' Man's inhumanity to man ' accounts for the nick-names that owe their origin to physical features. The nationals of every country have received such nicknames from the nationals of other countries. In every type of nickname, indeed, the Jews have merely shared the fate of the British and the French, the Germans and the Chinese. The prominent nose has produced the nicknames *hook-nose* (rare in the British Empire) and *schnozzle*, with the fanciful elaboration *schnozzola* (or *snozzola*) ; *schnozzle* is common in slang for any sort of nose and is, I am told, of Yiddish origin ; it has Latin antecedents, as we perceive from the fact that *Naso* (from Latin *nasus*, nose) is far from rare, as a cognomen among the Romans ; the poet Ovid always referred to himself as ' Naso '. Shakespeare makes the pedantic Holofernes say, in *Love's Labour's Lost*, ' And why, indeed, Naso, but for smelling out the odoriferous flowers of fancy . . . ? ' Caesar, perhaps the greatest man that ever lived, had a prominent nose. It is often a sign of character. Then there is *sheeny*, which probably refers to the shiny complexion and glossy hair of many Jews (not alone in the possession of these characteristics), although the word may, as Ernest Weekley proposes, spring from the ' Yiddish pronunciation of German *schön*, beautiful, used in praising wares '. *Sheeny*, an old term, in either interpretation is free of the offensiveness of the American nickname for Mexicans—*greasers* or *grease-balls*.

Closely allied to that group of nicknames is the group relating to religious and social habits. Americans speak of *herring-punishers* and *porkers*, with reference to the Jewish

12

dislike of pork and to their alleged addiction to herrings. American nicknames tend to be more personal, more callous than British. Another American term is *cloak-and-suiter*, with a glance at the large number of Jewish dealers in second-hand clothes. *Shonk* may belong to this group.

A more interesting group, philologically, is that formed by rhyming slang. Obviously *teapot lid* and *non-skid*, Cockney terms, rhyme with *Yid*. No less obviously, the British *buckle my shoe* and *four by two* (with the variant *three by two*) and the American *box of glue* and *fifteen two* rhyme with *Jew*. Less obvious, however, are two other American nicknames. Probably *goose* has been suggested by *Jewish* in its American shape, *Joosh*; and probably *kike* rhymes with *Ike*. *Kike* is a somewhat objectionable term, mainly because of its associations with the underworld.

But there always remains a list of unclassifiables. The Americans use *Arab*, presumably in ironic allusion to the centuries-old opposition between the two races; and *mockie* and *motzer*, which are of Yiddish origin, the latter deriving from Jewish ritual connected with the Passover. Both British and Americans use *smous* (or *smouse*), often varied to *smouch*, which may possibly come from ' Moses ' but more probably comes from *schmus*, ' patter ; profit ' (from a Hebrew word meaning ' tales, news ')—compare the Afrikaans *smouse*, ' a pedlar '. Both Americans and British employ, in one form or other, that term which occurs in at least four shapes—*shon* ; *shonk* ; *shonky* (or *shonkey*) ; *shonnicker* (or *shonniker* or *shonnacker*). The original form is *shonnicker*, a Yiddish word (meaning ' trader ' ?) ; whence, by compression, *shonk*, which yields a shortening, *shon*, and a diminutive, *shonky*.

It looks, therefore, as though the old best-wearing nicknames for Jews have been coined by the Jews themselves.

WORDS AT WAR : WORDS AT PEACE

Much as the best jokes against Jews and Scotchmen have been invented by—Jews and Scotchmen. A sense of humour is one of the three great social virtues. The Jews have it.

(Written in September, and published in
The Jewish Outlook in November, 1946.)

14

' *Aryan* ' and ' *Semitic* '

SEVERAL weeks after I received an invitation to write
this article, I came, purely by chance, upon this entry,
penned in July 1937, and included in the second edition
(1938, February) of my *Dictionary of Slang* : ' *Aryan* ; *non-
Aryan* ; non-Jewish ; Jewish : catachresis (of Hitlerite
origin) dating, in England, from 1936. This is a particularly crass and barbarous misusage of a useful pair of
complementaries.' A year later, Mr Patrick Carleton,
historian of the prehistoric Near East, was moved to
declare that ' probably no two technical terms have been
so consistently and hopelessly misused as the words *Semite*
and *Aryan* '. An odd coincidence. Or is it ? For ten years
now, all the judicious and the sensible among the human
race—and not merely the purists and the philologists—
have been protesting against this result of Hitler's absurd
Rassentheorie and his myth, both of them borrowed from
Rosenberg's *The Myth of the Twentieth Century*, 1930, of the
racial purity of German blood ; or, as a trenchant wit
phrased it, ' the bloody purity of the German race '.

Semitic, however, has caused rather less trouble than
Aryan. So let us glance at *Semitic* before we look at *Aryan*.

The current opinion among ethnologists and historians
is that there never has been a distinct Semitic race. What
concerns us here is that the Semitic language group—' the
Semitic family of languages '—is, very decidedly, a distinct and distinctive group ; these languages, very closely
inter-related, form a compact, homogeneous group, and a
Semite is a person that speaks one of these languages. It is

15

not going too far to say also that a Semite is one who, speaking a Semitic language, has religious beliefs and principles that appear to be inseparable from the use of such a language. To claim more is to fall into the same sort of error as that which we condemn in those who mis-use *Aryan*. In other words, we cannot have it both ways : either we should feel content to muddle along with the misuse of both *Semitic* and *Aryan* or we should apply, to the use of *Semitic*, principles no less strict than those we apply to the use of *Aryan*. Yet many people virtuously indignant at *Aryan* misused, are wonderfully complacent about *Semitic* misused.

The Semitic languages fall into two divisions. The older one, the East Semitic ; Akkadian, Assyrian, Babylonian, most intimately related one to the other. The younger or West Semitic, itself sub-divided into North-West Semitic (Hebrew, Aramaic, Syriac, etc.) and South-West Semitic (especially Arabic, Ethiopic, the present Abyssinian dia-lects). These Semitic languages, no matter which division or subdivision they belong to, are all far more closely inter-related than the languages of the so-called Aryan, or Indo-European, family are among themselves. Compare, for example, the Assyrian *Ilu*, the Hebrew *El*, the Arabic *Allah* : God.

The word *Semite* (whence, obviously, *Semitic*) comes, via German *semitisch*, from Modern Latin *Semita*, itself from Late Latin *Sem*, Greek *Sem*, i.e. *Shem*, a descendant of Shem, the eldest son of Noah. To try to go further than that is philologically foolish, because apparently related words in Hebrew may derive from the Hebrew for *Shem* rather than *Shem* from any of those other words. It is sometimes impossible to decide which of a Proper Name and a common noun (or adjective or verb) is the original.

Aryan presents greater difficulties : for one thing, it is, in its origin, Aryan or Indo-European, not Semitic ; and therefore, complicated, intricate relationships, as opposed to the simple Semitic inter-relationships, are involved. A modern shape of the basic root-word is *Iran*, with which compare *Areia*, the classical Greek word for Eastern Persia. Areia is, literally, ' noble land or country ' ; precisely as, I believe, Greek *aristos* (' best '), the source of our *aristocracy*, is literally ' noblest '. Now *Areia* comes, probably via Old Persian *Ariya* (a national name), from the Sanskrit *arya*, ' noble '. In the earliest Sanskrit, *arya* designated ' a worshipper of the Brahman God '—one of the Lords Spiritual, as it were—and was likewise a national name.

Somewhere about 1500 B.C., India was being invaded and conquered by that race which, originally migrants from Europe, we call the Aryans. The Aryans settled in India. And so we find a double movement, Europeans racially invading and dominating India and then, after some centuries, the Aryan language of India invading and dominating Europe—and, *en route*, certain Asiatic countries lying between North-Western India and Eastern Europe. The Aryans entered Western India perhaps from the west, perhaps from the north-east. We do not yet know for certain. The people they subdued were *non-Aryan* (in its literal, its proper, its strict sense) both racially and linguistically, and the Aryans called them ' the hostile-talking ', much as the Greeks later called all foreigners *barbaroi* (whence our *barbarians*), meaning literally ' the talkers of gibberish ; the stammerers ' and possessing an exact parallel in *Tartars* or *Tatars*. To the conquered race as a whole, the Aryans gave the name *Panis* or *Dasas*; and, derivatively, *Dasa*, in its feminine form *Dasi*, became the

17

name for a female slave, much as medieval Latin *Sclavus*, ' a Slav captive '—became our word *slave*.

Strictly, *Aryan* should be used only of those remote European invaders of India (and, by the way, Persia)—or of their language. That language forms one of a group spoken from Britain and Western Europe to India : and, by a natural and still permissible extension, its name, *Aryan*, has come to be applied to all the languages in this, the most remarkable of all language-groups, whether these languages belonged to the west Aryan sub-division (most of the European tongues) or to the East Aryan (Sanskrit, Persian, and the Hindi vernaculars). Philologically, *Aryan* is, even now, employed almost as often as the preferable *Indo-European* ; both of these terms, however, are preferable to *Indo-Germanic*, which we owe to the arrogance of those otherwise fine scholars, the great German comparative philologists of the 19th century. There is nothing Germanic about Greek or Latin ; much that is essentially European.

It was Max Muller (1823–1900) who, a German-born resident at Oxford from 1848 onwards, bestowed the name *Aryan* upon this family of languages. Later, he became the world's leading scholar in Oriental languages and retracted the theory, fathered by him, that the Aryan invaders of India were the Urvolk (primitive, or first, race) of the world ; he admitted that *Aryan* could not be applied to skull or hair, bones or skin or blood. Wholly false is the theory that the original Aryans, the invaders of Persia and India, belonged necessarily to the Nordic racial group, a group characterized by fair hair and skin, large bones and long, narrow skulls. ' There is ', said Patrick Carleton in 1939, ' no possible proof—that is, possible at present—of the still wilder theory which would make of these (imagin-

ary) " Proto-Aryans " a race of supermen, the founders of
European culture, whose " racially pure " descendants
are the natural masters and rulers of all other peoples.'
Since that was written (actually in 1937) Nietzsche's
blond beasts have once more proved that their culture is
Kultur and that, so far from being *Herrenvolk* (' the master
race '), they are so little masters of themselves that they
allowed a crafty controller and utilizer of mass hysteria
to dominate them. So much for Aryan domination !

' As a matter of fact ', wrote Walter Theimer in his
admirable *Political Dictionary* (December 1939) ' there is
no such thing as an Aryan in Europe. The myth, however, has survived its creator (Max Muller) and become
the principal weapon of Anti-Semitism. Thus " Aryan " is
often merely synonymous with " non-Jewish " ! '

To which we must, in fairness, add the pronouncement
made by Patrick Carleton in *Buried Empires*. ' The fact of
the matter is that we are no more able to speak of an
" Indogermanic race " than of a " Semitic race ".' But
we can, with reservations, speak of ' Aryan languages ' ;
and of ' Semitic languages ' with no reservation at all.

(Written in August, and published in
The Jewish Outlook in September, 1946.)

19

The Language of Palmistry

IN the autumn of 1916, a tentful of Anzacs at Etaples were sent to isolation camp because one of them had caught some childish complaint—German measles, probably. And were we pleased, or were we ? It was, after September, an unpleasant autumn, hinting at that bitter winter which every old soldier remembers with a shiver.

It was not a martinet camp, as we immediately perceived. Perceiving, we sent off to Messrs Hatchard a weird collection of chicken-feed French currency-notes and asked for almost as weird a collection of books. A young sheep-farmer (an excellent lawn-tennis player) had the odd idea that he wanted to study palmistry : his fate was to be taken prisoner at Lagnicourt four months later, with another member of the same tentful—a Scotsman, who had ordered a history of Scotland. He studied ; became enthusiastic ; infected me with his enthusiasm. I conned the book, which was one of Cheiro's smaller works on palmistry. We practised on the other members of the group, and on ourselves, and became astonishingly expert. I kept up palmistry for seven or eight years, and had much fun with it. There is far more ' to it ' than fun, especially in the character-reading part ; in the prophecies, I confess, I haven't much faith, for even if (as they may be) they are well founded, accident and chance so often render them invalid or, rather, inoperative.

Cheiro, by far the best known writer on palmistry, was Count Louis Hamon. Besides a *Guide to the Hand* and *Palmistry for All*, he wrote an extremely popular *Book of*

Numbers, of which I know nothing but which I suspect to have been tongue-in-the-cheekish, and *Cheiro's Language of the Hand*, his longest and most important book on palmistry. Published in 1895, the *Language* reached its 15th edition in 1912, its 26th in 1938. In the *Preface* and *Defense*, Cheiro remarks that ' in the remotest period of the Aryan civilization, palmistry had even a literature of its own ' and that ' in the northwest province of India palmistry was practised and followed by the Joshi caste from time immemorial ' ; the Greeks took it up ; the Jews studied it. In *The Book of Job*, there is a verse (xxxvii, 7) that, in at least one translation (not that of the English Bible), runs, ' God placed signs or seals in the hands of men, that all men might know their works ', in which, according to at least one interpretation, the ' signs and seals ' are the lines, mounts, and other markings— and these, ' the markings of God, that all men might know their works '. Certain less attested theories and beliefs have millions of supporters and devotees ; and many scientists have emphasized the significance of the markings on the hand. Some scientists have indeed gone so far as to assert that ' the brain cannot think without the hand feeling the influence of the thought ' ; that is as may be, but it is fairly generally admitted that ' as the hands are the servants of the (bodily) system, so all that affects the system affects them ' and that there are more nerves between the brain and the hand than between the brain and any other part of the body. Moreover, ' the hand, by its direct communication with every portion of the brain, tells not only the qualities active, but those dor-mant, and those which will be developed ' (Cheiro).

But to come to the language of palmistry.

Palmistry is a poor term ; it is, however, the generally

accepted one. It means ' art or skill of the palm ' ; that is, the art of (or, skill in) reading the palm of the hand. But far more than the palm is read : the whole hand is studied in its general conformation, in the shape of the thumb and fingers and even the kind of nails, in the mounts (or mounds), as well as in the lines and other markings on the palm. Of the other terms for the study of the hand—terms all based on the Greek *cheir*, ' the hand ' (in combination, usually in the form *chir*)—only *chirology*, ' hand lore ', is satisfactory, for it includes both character-reading and fortune-telling ; *chirognomy* (' hand-knowing ') refers only to the former, *chiromancy* (' hand-divination ') only to the latter. The corresponding agents or practitioners are known as *palmists, chirologists, chirognomists*, and *chiromancers*.

More interesting, more romantic, more storied than those general terms are the terms designating the mounts and lines ; the girdles, bracelets and rings, the stars and the crosses ; the islands ; the squares and the circles ; the triangles and the quadrangles ; yea, and the grilles.

Even the shapes or types of hand are named in a manner that arouses curiosity. These are the *elementary*, or lowest, and the *psychic* or *idealistic*, the highest type ; the *square*, or useful ; the *spatulate* (from Latin *spatula*, the diminutive of *spatha*, ' a broad blade '), which is the nervous, energetic type ; the *knotty*, or philosophic type ; the *conic*, or artistic ; and the *mixed* hand, belonging to the versatile—and the changeable.

The *mounts* are, in the main, those fleshy mounds or prominences which are at the base of the thumb and fingers. (I follow Cheiro in refraining from giving to these names those senses which they possessed in the exploded superstition known as Astrological Palmistry.) The *mons*

22

Veneris or *mount of Venus* is the prominence or mound at the base of the thumb. Relating to the goddess of love, it is, when not abnormally large, a favourable sign, for then it denotes affection, sympathy, benevolence, a desire to please, and a love of beauty in Nature, art, literature, music. When very large, it indicates an intense liking for the opposite sex. It is not to be confused with the *girdle of Venus*. The other mounds are these :—The *mons Jovis* or *mount of Jupiter*, which, situated at the base of the first finger, indicates the degree of ambition, desire for power, pride, enthusiasm for anything attempted ; the *mons Saturni* or *mount of Saturn*, at the base of the second (the longest) finger and, if highly developed, showing prudence, earnestness, love of solitude and serious study, and, in the musical, an appreciation of sacred and classical music ; the *mons solis* or *mount of the sun*, which, at the base of the third (or ring) finger, is also called the *mount of Apollo*, Apollo being the sun-god of the Greeks and Romans as well as the patron of music and poetry, and when this mount is well developed ' it indicates an enthusiastic appreciation of all things beautiful, whether or not one follows a purely artistic calling ' (Cheiro) ; the *mons Mercurii* or *mount of Mercury*, which, at the base of the little finger, stands for the mercurial qualities, such as love of change and excitement, wittiness and quick wits. There are three other mounds : two named *mons Martis* or *mount of Mars*, the one situated beneath the mount of Jupiter and lying next to the mount of Venus, and the other, lying between the mounts of Mercury and Luna ; the third, the *mons lunae* or mount of the moon, being on the side of the hand, beneath the mount of Mars and opposite the mount of Venus. If two mounts lean towards each other, their qualities are blended.

The lines—paramount, but modified by the other manual features—are fourteen in number; seven main and seven subsidiary. The lesser lines are the *line of Mars*, *of marriage*, *of intuition*, the *via lasciva* (or line of inordinate sexuality), and the three *bracelets* found on the wrist. The seven greater lines are the *line of life*, or *vital line*; the *line of the head*, or *cerebral* (or *natural*) *line*; the *line of the heart*, or *mensal line* in Cheiro's nomenclature, though *The Oxford Dictionary* gives it as an alternative name for the *line of fate* or *fortune* or *destiny*, otherwise known as the *line of Saturn* (or *Saturnian line*); the *line of health*, or *liver line* or *via hepatica*; the *line of Apollo* or *brilliance* or *the sun*; and the *girdle of Venus*, which, unless it is found on a broad, thick hand, does not (as generally supposed) indicate sensuality, but rather sensitiveness, great intelligence, also touchiness and a highly strung temperament.

Finally there are the less known markings. The *ring of Saturn*, which is rare, denotes big ideas linked with infirmity of purpose; it interrupts the line of fate. Various *stars* are significant, especially those on the mounts, for instance that on the mount of Saturn is fate-fraught destiny-directed, whereas that on the mount of Venus is fortunate (*bonnes fortunes*). *Squares* are numerous and usually called 'the marks of preservation'—preservation from actual danger or from a dangerous tendency connoted by some line or mount. *Crosses* are seldom favourable; the most important exception is the cross on the mount of Jupiter, a cross that indicates that 'at least one great affection will come into the life'. An *island* is unfortunate, though only in the restricted field of that marking in conjunction with which it is found. The one *circle* that is propitious is the circle on the mount of

Apollo or the sun. *Spots* are signs of a temporary illness, injury, or nervous shock. *Grilles* (or networks) denote obstacles to the potentiality of that mount on which they are found. The lesser *triangles*, occurring on the mounts, are of good omen. The *great triangle* (the *triangle of Mars*), formed by the lines of life, head, and health, is excellent if large ; if small, it shows timidity, meanness, cowardice. The *quadrangle*, situated between the lines of head and heart, is favourable or unfavourable, according to certain variations. The *croix mystique* (or *mystic cross*) lies within that quadrangle and, if clearly marked, it indicates superstitiousness or, at its best, mysticism. The *ring of Solomon* is ' a sign that also denotes the love of the occult, but . . . it shows more the power of the master, the adept, than the mere love of the mystic denoted by " La Croix Mystique " ' (Cheiro).

Such are the most important markings and their names ; such, very briefly indeed, are their meanings. There are legends and ancient lore, numerous ramifications and subtle modifications, but they cannot be treated here. Chirology was not formulated in a day, nor can it be learnt in a month. The terminology, however, is less difficult, especially to a word-lover.

(Written in 1938.)

Note. The writer is a scholar, not a palmist : and, in his ignorance, he cannot answer inquiries about palmistry.

You Takes Yer Choice

VAGARIES OF COLOUR

'PENNY plain, twopence coloured'. Plain : black and white. Coloured : the other hues.

In all European languages, adjectives and nouns of colour have their transferred, their metaphorical senses. The French Symbolist, Rimbaud, wrote a well-known poem, *The Vowels*, which begins, ' Ye vowels, *A* black, *E* white, *I* red, *U* green, *O* blue ' : idiom has never caught up with that symbolism ; but it is nevertheless rich in metaphor. With the private notations of poets, we are hardly concerned, although we may recall those verses in Swinburne's *Madonna Mia* which run :

> Only this thing is said,
> That white and gold and red,
> God's three chief words, man's bread
> And oil and wine,
> Were given her for dowers.

At the opposite end of the scale is this piece of colour superstition from the folk-lore of the East of England :

> Blue is true,
> Yellow is jealous,
> Green's forsaken,
> Red's brazen,
> White is love,
> And black is death.

' Penny plain ' : white and black. *White* is often regarded as the absence of colour—and as the opposite of *black* ; hence as the absence of stain (' the world's slow stain ')—cleanness—purity.

> Life is a sheet of paper *white*
> Whereon each one of us may write
> His word or two : and then comes night :

late-19th-century verses in imitation of the famous French poem, *La vie est vaine*, itself an imitation of a forgotten French poem of the mid-19th century. ' Wearing the *white* flower of a *blameless* life ', the pure (as Tennyson there implies) are held to subscribe to Swinburne's antithesis of

> The *lilies* and languors of virtue,
> The raptures and *roses* of vice.

Then there is Beaumont & Fletcher's ' a soul as white as heaven '. From such thoughts as these, idiom has evolved the phrase *white virtue*, in the sense of negative virtue : virtue untried, untempted : as in Hugh Kimber's arresting novel, *White Virtue*. But not always nor necessarily untried, unproved : in a poem to Walter Savage Landor, Swinburne, though riotously pagan as are so many weaklings in revolt against their own impotence, could speak of

> The darkling day that gave its blood-red birth
> To Milton's *white* republic *undefiled*.

Virtue is often associated with the cloistered life (' A fugitive and cloistered virtue ' is Milton's eloquent phrase in perhaps the most eloquent passage in that clarion-call to liberty of speech, *Areopagitica*), a life that often undermines energy of character, sharpness of decision :

> And thus the native hue of resolution
> Is *sicklied* o'er with the *pale* cast of thought :
> (*Hamlet*)

27

In *white nights* (adopted from France : *nuits blanches*) there is a fusion of two ideas : virtuous *white* and the whiteness cast by the lit lamp of sleeplessness. Pallor of study ; pallor of insomnia ; pallor of fear. The *white-livered* person flags the *white feather* given by crass girls to officers in mufti, even to retired V.C.'s. And *white* is also the banner of old age : ' Their winters *white* as faith's and age's hue ' (Swinburne). *White* magic is beneficent, *black* magic is maleficent.

Black connotes, above all, iniquity, foulness, crime. Greene, that Elizabethan ' *black* sheep ', confesses, in *Greene's Groatsworth of Wit*, that ' *Black* is the remembrance of my *black* works ' ; Feilding mentions ' Concealing facts of the *blackest* dye ' ; *black mass* has become synonymous with ritualistic foulness. From crime to the reprobation with which it is regarded is but a short step : ' to get into a person's *black* books ' or ' to be put on the *black* list ' is always unpleasant ; so, also, to be treated with the ' *black* looks ' of anger (' The monks looked *black* ', writes Browning). Not only of anger but of melancholy. ' To be in a *black* mood, or a *black* humour ' is to feel depressed —perhaps for no better reason than a black sky.

A more vivid group consists of *red* and *pink, rose* and *rosy blushing, crimson, purple, puce. Red* has three main connotations. The first is that of blood : ' *red* War ' and ' Nature, *red* in tooth and claw ' (Tennyson). Associated with this is, the juxtaposition of *redness* and Socialism, a Socialist being a *Red*. Older and more basic is the *red* of youth and love.

> Upon her raiment of dyed sendaline
> Were painted all the secret ways of love
> And covered things thereof
> That hold delight as grape-flowers hold their wine ;
> *Red* mouths of maidens and *red* feet of doves,

28

as Swinburne has it in A *Ballad of Death*, with perhaps a covert allusion to the doves of Venus's car.

Rose and *rosy* also are connected with the imagery of love and youth : youthful love : middle-aged love : agèd love, the most pathetic. ' With a smile that glow'd Celestial rosy red, love's proper hue ', writes Milton (not inexpert in the lore of love) in *Paradise Lost*. *Rosy* cheeks, flushed with youth or love or both, are offensive to the dragons of virtue and to the envious ; Richard Aldington, in *Women Must Work*, alludes to a dowager that could not abide girls because of their ' horrid bloom '. ' English *Rose* ' is synonymous with English girlhood and early womanhood. Or should I not rather say, with British ? Burns lyricizes thus : ' Oh, my love's like a red, red rose— That's newly sprung in June ' ; and Akenside speaks of ' the *rosy* breath of love '. With youth and with love are associated the flushed cheeks of sleep : ' Her *rosy* slumbers shall not fly ' (Sheridan). And there are the flushed cheeks of the inspired orator : ' *rosy* eloquence ' (Keats). Rosy blushes : ' *Blushing* is the colour of virtue ', says Mathew Henry in his commentary on *Jeremiah*. Compare Shakespeare's ' And bears his *blushing* honours thick upon him '.

Crimson is less fruitful in metaphor than one might suppose. Metaphorically it is notably connected only with blood ; figuratively it is synonymous with ' sanguinary ', as in ' *crimson* conquest ' (Sir William Jones) and ' *crimson* crime ' (Professor Blackie). Hence, in slang, *crimson* and *sanguinary* are euphemisms and facetiousnesses for ' bloody '. *Pink*, however, has a rich synonymy. It is used of the flower—the finest exemplar—of excellence, as in ' I am the very *pink* of courtesy ' (*Romeo and Juliet*) and ' In the very *pink* of the mode ' (Thackeray). Whence springs the delightful *in the pink*, ' in excellent health and pink cheeks ' as some forgotten wit has phrased it : ' I am in the pink ', says—unblushingly—a Tommy that is far from being in that rude, robust condition ; indeed, an authenticated instance runs, ' This comes hoping it will find you in the pink as it leaves me with scabies '. From exuberant health, spring ribaldry and rich vulgarity : *pink* has occasionally been employed to denote ' slightly vulgar, or slightly indecent ' ; in *The Daily News* of 1900 (I take this, and certain other of my examples, from *The O.E.D.*) there occurs the sentence, ' Most of their adjectives have a decidedly *pink* tinge '. And owing to the influence of *red*, ' Socialistic ', we have *pink* derivatively used of mild Socialism.

On our way to *blue*, we encounter *puce* and *purple*. The former is a slang term for ' objectionable ' : perhaps by association with the colour of blood-gorged lice, as in ' That was a *lousy* trick to play on you ! ' *Purple* is much more dignified. Purple is the distinguishing colour of kings and emperors : *born in the purple, cradled in the purple* bear witness to the imperiality of purple. ' A truly imperial prose ' is a phrase used by that great stylist, Frank Binder : a prose, not of ' *purple* patches, pieces and passages ' but of majestic impressiveness. The earliest form of these rhetorical references is *purple patch*, which was originally a translation of *purpureus pannus*, occurring in that quint-essence and vade-mecum of literary good-sense, Horace's *Ars Poetica* ; the least used is *purple piece* ; *purple passage*, the most. Donning the purple again, we find the inter-esting colloquialism, ' to have a *purple* time of it ', which is equivalent to the more usual ' have a *royal* time of it '. *Purple*, in two of its senses, however, approximates to *red* and *rosy* : to the former in ' He is come to open the *purple* testament of bleeding war ' (*Richard II*) ; to the latter in ' The bloom of young Desire and *purple* light of love ' (Gray, *The Progress of Poesy*).

Purple represents a fusion of red and *blue*. ' *Blue* blood ' indicates noble birth. Aristocratic, perhaps, is the association of blue with constancy, as in *true blue* ; aristocratic, certainly, is the association with Conservatism. Allied is that *blue* which denotes ' genuine ', ' stirling ' : an almost forgotten proverb tells us that ' True blue will never stain '. Intense cold produces blue hands ; the accompanying physical state leads readily to a devitalized feeling ; that feeling to a mood of depression. We speak of ' having the *blues* ', Disraeli once admitted that ' Even the knowing ones look blue ', and Frank L. Stanton sings, ' Just a-wearyin' for you—All the time a-feelin' blue '. From depression it is far too easy to sink to fear ; ' one gets in a *blue* funk ', a phrase wherein *blue* is not only metaphorical but intensive. It is purely intensive in ' to cry (or shout) *blue* murder '. The sense ' pedantic ', ' learned ', as applied to women (' *Blue* ladies there are in Boston ', as Dickens found), comes from *blue stocking*, ' a learned female ' : in the 18th century, there appeared at certain literary salons presided over by women and much frequented by them, a young intellectual and poet that wore blue stockings : whence, by easy stages, the term *blue stockings* for the learned ladies. Moribund is the slangy sense ' indecent, obscene ', which may have arisen partly from sulphurous oaths (' The air was *blue* with curses ') and partly from *La Bibliothèque Bleue*, a series of books, some of which were rather *Oh, là, là !* But the association of *blue* with sailors and the sea has endured, as in ' the *blue*-water school ' and ' our boys in *blue* ', though admittedly both of these phrases are somewhat

31

fly-blown ; but the shipping-company posters do not allow us to forget ' the *blue* Mediterranean ', despite the fact that the inland sea is often blue-grey or even uncontradictably grey.

Grey hair of advancing age ; *grey* eyes of quietude ; *grey* skies of Britain. ' Is *grey* experience suited to her youth ? ' asks Sheridan ; ' *Gray* wisdom comes with time and age ', wisely says that master platitudinist, Lewis Morris. In ' Her locks covered with *grey* despair ' (William Blake) and ' His face was full of *grey* old miseries ' (Swinburne) we have the transition to the metaphorical senses, ' depressing, sad, dismal, gloomy ', further exemplified in ' The student who stays at home and learns in a *gray* way only from books ', as Professor Blackie, who often turned the tables on his own students, contemptuously puts it.

Theirs was ' a *brown* study ', I presume. To many of us, the phrase *brown study* seems odd. Why *brown*? But *brown* once had the transferred meanings, ' dusky ', as in Pope's ' Or ere *brown* evening spread her chilly shade ' ; hence ' gloomy ' ; hence ' serious ' or ' gloomily serious ', —and ' gloomily serious ' is the exact sense connoted in *brown study*. Related is *golden*, which is yellowy and either sunnily or lambently brown.

> See *golden* days, fruitful of *golden* deeds,
> With joy and love triumphing,

sings Milton ; ' I learned the first part in my *golden* age ', says Walton, who thus refers back to the Golden Age, when all were happy, sin flourished not, but culture did, and perhaps also to the use of *golden* for young men and women of fair looks and lusty health, as in Shakespeare's

> *Golden* lads and girls all must
> As chimney-sweepers come to dust,

which makes one think of those golden girls of the 1890's (*The Quest of the Golden Girl*, Richard Le Gallienne's most famous novel). Then there are the associations of ' the *Golden* West ' : the goldfields of California ; the sun sinking in western gold.

So to *yellow*, which has four distinct associations : age ; cowardice ; unscrupulous sensationalism ; jealousy. ' My way of life ', says regretful Macbeth, ' Is fall'n into the sere, the *yellow* leaf '. The yellowness of age is often compared to old and wrinkled parchment. The connotation of cowardice is modern. The phrase ' He's yellow ' means that ' He is a coward, despite an outward show of courage '. In ' the *Yellow Press* ', the adjective satirizes the tendency of certain American (and, latterly, English) newspapers to exploit sensationalism and sentiment in a nauseatingly unscrupulous manner ; it arises from an illustration (' The Yellow Kid ') designed, most successfully, in 1895 to attract purchasers. In the 17th–18th centuries it was customary to say ' *yellow* with jealousy ', especially in reference to the emotion aroused in a cuckold. By an easy transition via *yellowish green* and by a cast-back to Shakespeare's ' O, beware, my lord, of jealousy ! It is the green-eyed monster which doth mock the meat it feeds on ' (compare, perhaps, Shakespeare's ' With a *green and yellow* melancholy, She sat like patience on a monument, Smiling at grief '), we now, as they did in the 19th century, say *green with envy* and *green with jealousy*.

Thus have we arrived at *green*, the last colour to be here dealt with. *Green* means ' full of vitality ', as in ' a *green* old age '. Hence it is applied to a vigorous memory : ' The memory be *green* ' occurs in *Hamlet* ; in Austin Dobson we hear of ' His still *green* recollections of that memorable night '. It is, inevitably, applied to the young : ' *Green* pleasure and grey grief ' is a neat antithesis in Swinburne's *A Match*. And, derivatively, to the spiritually young : ' Though grey our heads, our thoughts and aims are *green* ', writes the was-he-ever Young. Derivatively also is it used of immaturity : ' *Green* probationers in mischief ', observed Lamb with his unquenchable twinkle ; ' But these are *green* resolves ', says George Eliot. A link with the further derivative sense, ' gullible ', comes in the epigram, ' Ladies who are very blue are apt to be rather *green* ' (Westmacott) ; a sense that belongs to unconventional speech : ' Do you see any *green* in my eye ? ' is a catch-phrase, with the variant, ' I'm not so *green* as I'm cabbage-looking '.

There are other colours : *violet* (so modest !), *buff* (stripped to the), *fawn*, *amaranthine* (' the amaranthine flower of faith ', Wordsworth), *orange*, and the rest of them. But this article isn't a spectrum : and exhaustiveness conduces to exhaustion.

(Written early in 1939 and published in
John o' London's Weekly, 1939.)

34

Silk, Tartars and Barbarians

IN 1936, the famous Swedish explorer in Asia, the notable geographer, Sven Anders Hedin (born so long ago as 1865), who also wrote such very readable books as *Across the Gobi Desert, From Pole to Pole*, and *The Wandering Lake*, brought out *The Silk Road*. Sven Hedin, who travelled in Persia and Mesopotamia at the age of 20–21 ; in Khurasan and Turkestan in 1890–91, and from Orenburg to Peiping in the next few years ; in the Gobi Desert in 1899–1902 ; in Tibet during the same period and again later ; and, hearty old man, was a member of the Swedish expedition in China in 1926–33 : Sven Hedin, who wrote almost as interestingly as he explored intrepidly, has in *The Silk Road* given us the best account of that great highway. (Or rather, highways : for there were probably two main ' silk roads '. And both *highway* and *road* are misleading : *route* would be a more accurate term.) Like Marco Polo, probably the world's greatest traveller, who had, six hundred years earlier, passed through many of the countries that the Swedish explorer came to know so well, Sven Hedin writes realistically, though not with the genius of a Sir Richard Burton or a Doughty, nor yet with the talent of a St John Philby or a Peter Fleming. What makes Sven Hedin and Marco Polo such good reading is their resourcefulness, their courage, the sharpness of their observation, the intimacy as well as the exactitude of their knowledge. That, after 1933, Sven Hedin fell under the spell of Nazism, is not to his credit : but this is a fact irrelevant to the worth of his geographical achievements.

The Silk Road, whether the Northern or the Southern Route, started from northern or central China, kept north of Tibet (mainly) and of India (entirely), and passed through northern Persia, to end in Asia Minor and Syria. That is to state a stirring and romantic business so baldly as to put it badly. In *The Silk Road*, Sven Hedin invests the subject with the historical details necessary to its understanding and with the colour that is its due, and to all those who can bear to have information conveyed excitingly, and adventure mixed with erudition (the latter cunningly concealed), and geography blended with history—and human nature with both—to all those, I recommend *The Silk Road*.

There is, however, a caution to be added. Not to Sven Hedin, but to the preceding and consequent matter in this essay. In the period before Christ and probably for some centuries after His death, there was almost certainly—from Central Asia onwards, at the least—one main silk road, and one only, leading from China to Asia Minor and Syria. Several routes from China converged until they met at Kashgar or at Yarkand, or further west at Khokand or more probably at Samarkand ; continued as one until they reached some point immediately south of the Caspian, whence one or two routes descended through Persia while another proceeded west to Aleppo, whence one ' carried on ' into Asia Minor and another forked south, through Syria and Palestine, to Alexandria. The caravans to India probably went, either from Kashgar or Yarkand or from Khokand or Samarkand, south through Afghanistan. But at some early period A.D. ' the " Turks " came to " High Tartary " from the steppes of Northern Mongolia, and found Zungaria a much richer land than their old home. . . . In the early days the rich and fertile Hwang-ho basin

was " very near ", and supplied all that the raiding
instincts of the tribes wanted ; and it was even the Hun
control of the *natural* Silk Route *via* Hami and Umrutsi
that forced the Chinese to find the *unnatural* ones along
the northern and the—still safer—southern margin of the
Tarim basin ' (Lionel W. Lyde, *The Continent of Asia*) :
hence the medieval North and South Silk Roads.

We know that Chinese silk had reached India before
Alexander the Great invaded it in 327 B.C. ' Then in
115 B.C. under the Han Dynasty the Chinese army occupied, albeit only temporarily, the Tarim basin. At length
the civilizations of the Far East and the Near East were
in contact directly, no longer through intermediaries. . . .
After 115 the silk caravans, equipped by the Empire,
travelled on roads protected by blockhouses and police.
. . . After 114 B.C. a dozen caravans a year loaded with
silks crossed the deserts of Central Asia from China to
Russian Turkestan, whence the fashionable stuff was sent
to Seleucia, Antioch, Alexandria and Rome,' as Professor
V. Gordon Childe recalls in his alert and informative
What Happened in History.

Early Europe knew of China, either as two lands or as
one land with two names, the one being Greek and the
other Chinese. The northern land was *Seres*, the southern
Sin—with such variant forms as *Sinoe, Ch'in, China*. The
First Dynasty of China was the Ch'in Dynasty. The
people were the Ch'ins—' *the* Men ', the master-race of
that time and that part of the world. ' From the eighth
century B.C.', remarks Professor Lionel W. Lyde in his
fascinating book, *The Continent of Asia* (geography, not
history), ' a principality of this name was in complete
control of the Chinese and of the Zungarian gateways to
and from the West, and it gradually spread southward

37

through the Red Basin, until in the fourth century it had control also of the Yangtze link with the Irawadi. This was at the very time when Persia, on the Indus and the Amu, was controlling the western ends of both of these lines of approach, and from this time onward Ch'in ... completely controlled all natural intercourse between China and the West. ... Western Asia and Europe extended to the lands farther east—knowledge of which, and the products from which, they obtained only through and from Ch'in—the name of the great state that they did know directly'; and *Ch'in*, a region, became the vast region we call *China*.

The Arabs, the Persians, the Ayran-Indians, as well as the Greeks and the Romans, must have come to hear about, then to see and to handle, silk at a very early period. The Silk Roads were among the most used of the great and ancient caravan routes. 'Bhamo was a silk-market by the 7th century B.C., though the " Silk Road " may have developed out of a " Salt Trail " ' (Lyde). Two main lines of approach to China from the West, originally from China to the West, were, basically or at least virtually, Silk Roads. ' It is almost certain that the silk trade originated with the Tokharians, or Yue-chi ' (Lyde).

The English word *silk*, in its present form, dates back to the later Middle Ages, and in Middle English we find such forms as *silc*, *selc*, *seolk* or *seolc*, *seoloc* and *sioloc*, the last two being particularly significant. Those forms, which should be compared with Old Norse *silki* and Old Slavic (or Russian) *shelku*, are significant, because the ultimate source of *silk* is Latin *sericus* or Greek *serikos*, from Latin and Greek *Seres*, that Eastern people—presumably the Chinese—by whom silk was first exported and trans-ported to the West. The Greek, or maybe the Latin, word seems to have passed into Old Slavic through some language that confused *r* and *l* ; and from Russia, via the Baltic trade and perhaps also through Old Norse, it found its way into Old English.

The actual Greek word concerned would be *serikon*, the neuter of the adjective *serikos*, ' silken ', used as a noun ; whence the corresponding Latin *sericum*. The original sense of *serikos* is ' *Seric* '—of or belonging to the people known as the Seres ; from the little used singular, *Ser* (' one of the Seres ') came the second century (A.D.) Greek *ser*, ' a silkworm '. Since *serikos* means both ' of the Seres (or Chinese) ' and ' of silk ', it is obvious that *silk* is etymologically ' the *Seric*—that is, the *Chinese*—fabric or stuff or material '.

But which language was it that changed the *r* of *serikon* or *sericum* to an *l*, so that the ancient Russians, and finally the English, spelt the word with an *l* and, at the end, gave us *silk* ? We are dealing, remember, not with a Chinese word translated into Greek and Latin and then passed through Russia to Britain, but with a Greek word that did so. As Chinese merchants travelled west, so Greek and Roman merchants travelled east ; they met in Persia, in north-west India, even in Central Asia. What is more likely than that Chinese merchants, who travelled also, by a north-west route, into Russia, passed on, to the ancient Slavs, their version of the Greek word, *serikon*, or of the Latin one, *sericum* ? The Chinese inability (outside the Mandarin classes) to pronounce *r* and their consequent corruption of *r* to *l* (*velly* for *very*) are known to every schoolboy. Some of the pundits have made difficulties where difficulty did not exist !

Now, the Silk Roads—or one of them—passed through Tartary, or at least Chinese Tartary—although in B.C.

and early A.D. times the country was not so called, nor
were its inhabitants called *Tatars* or *Tartars*. These names
first became known to the West in their application to the
army of Genghiz Khan, who (in 1202–27) had under him
a medley of Mongols, Tatars, Turks, and who laid waste
much of Asia and Eastern Europe. Those three races are
closely interrelated : as Tartary stretches from the Caspian Sea, through what is now northern Persia and
Turkestan, then immediately north of Tibet, and as far
east as, and including, inner and outer Mongolia, so you
get a continual mixing of those three originally nomadic
races mentioned above. The Tatars are, ethnically, so
named because they spring from the Tata Mongols, who
in the 9th century migrated southward from the north-
eastern region of the Gobi and, driving before or with
them many tribesmen of Turkish stock, invaded Russia.
The Persian form is *Tatar*. But Western Europeans immediately referred to Genghiz Khan's brutal and all-
conquering hordes as *Tartari* (a latinized form) or *Tartares*
or *Tartars*, and the reason is twofold : even *Tata* is pronounced *tah-tah*, and the difference between the Conti-
nental pronunciation of *Tatar* (as *tah-tar*) and *Tartar* is
too slight for coarse ears ; moreover, Western Europeans
very naturally regarded the Khan's licentious soldiery as
' devils from Hell ' ; that is, as *Tartari* or inhabitants of
Tartarus (the Greek-mythological hell) ; in short, as
Tatars that were, if met, *Tartars*. Whence the phrase, *to
catch a Tartar*, which originally meant ' to encounter a foe
certainly as brave as, and probably fiercer than, oneself ' :
a Tatar strayed from that medieval army.

Probably predominant in Genghiz Khan's army were
these Tatars, who, as related above, had already
caused the Chinese merchants to go north and south of

the Tarim basin long before these silk-carriers could set a direct line for Kashgar or Samarkand. The Chinese, who had been an artistic and cultured race for more than a thousand years before the Tatars settled across the ancient Silk Road, gave to this uncouth people a name they had probably borrowed from the Persians : *Tata* or *Tatar* or perhaps *Tartar*, for in these matters we cannot afford to be dogmatic.

To the Chinese, though perhaps not to the Persians, the word *tata* (etc.) represented *ta-ta* (pronounced *tah-tah*) or *tartar* ; and that reduplication corresponds exactly with the *bar-bar* of *Barbaroi*, the name visited by the Greeks upon all those peoples who, not speaking Greek, were that most criminal of all things—foreigners. To the Greek, the Barbarians (*hoi barbaroi*) were ' talkers in— speakers of—the *bar-bar* language ' : the language of stammerers, the conversation of gibberers. To the Greek, by the way, the ancient Italians were as much barbarians as was any other foreign race. (Later the Italians came to apply *barbari* as a term of reproach to all those who spoke neither Latin nor Greek. And look at the way we, in our turn, use the term *barbarian* !) Ancient Greek is a musical tongue ; Greeks thought the languages they encountered to be unmusical, the speakers to be uncouth and bar- barous. So, too, the subtle, cultured Chinese thought the language of the Mongols ugly and stammeringly repetitive.

(Written in May 1946. My 1946 Christmas card.)

The World's Potted Wisdom

A MINOR pleasure of one's maturer years is proving for oneself the wisdom of ancient saws after having, in youth, doubted and even denied their applicability to modern instances. Dr Selwyn Champion's *Racial Proverbs* will not only increase that pleasure but also buttress one's growing conviction that in the potted wisdom of the world's proverb literature there is shrewdness, common sense, good sense, and at times a penetrating profundity ; humour and wit ; beneficent satire and expedient salvation.

Dr Champion's definition is this : ' A proverb is a racial aphorism which has been, or still is, in common use, conveying advice or counsel, invariably camouflaged figuratively, disguised in metaphor or allegory ' ; occasionally the metaphor is little, if anything, more than an epigrammatic point.

In his instructive introduction, the editor gives many of the various words for a proverb. (*Proverb* itself comes from the Latin.) In Arabic the corresponding term signifies a parable or a similitude ; in Chinese a common saying ; in Greek, a wayside saying—compare the English *by-word* ; in Japanese, words that work ; in Sanskrit, an excellent saying ; in Turkish, an ancestral saying. And he ushers-in this remarkable collection of the world's proverbs, admirably arranged and most legibly printed, with a number of proverbs and sayings concerning proverbs. Here are a few : ' A proverb says what man thinks ' (Swedish) ; ' Old sayings contain no lies '

42

(Basque) ; 'All the good sense of the world runs into proverbs' (English) ; 'As the people, so the proverb' (Scottish) ; 'As a country, so the morals ; as the morals, so the proverbs' (German) ; 'When a fool is told a proverb, the meaning has to be explained to him' (Oji).

Such proverbs are comparatively modern, but many proverbs are ancient : ' the sayings in *The Book of the Dead* were in general use in Egypt as far back as 3700 B.C. . . . Aristotle, one of the first known collectors of proverbs, more than 2,000 years ago spoke of them as " fragments of an elder wisdom " '. Many British proverbs are over a thousand years old. A small matter. Still smaller, from the viewpoint of date, is the collection of English-speaking Americans' proverbs, but from the viewpoint of force, these American proverbs are notable : witness ' Life is just one damned thing after another ', which a wit has amplified with ' And love, two damned things after each other '. (No ; Dr Champion does not record the amplification.)

Even more striking than the antiquity of proverbs is their number. There are, for instance, at least 225,000 German proverbs, and over 1,000,000 Finnish ; more than 60,000 Russian and 30,000 Swedish.

From the mass of material the editor has selected 26,000 of the best—the most significant—proverbs, drawn from 186 languages and dialects. And he has done it extraordinarily well.

The vast numbers he had to choose from do not comport a proportional variety. ' Proverbial wisdom ', he remarks, ' is exactly the same all the world over, differing only in rendering. " Men are all made of the same paste " (Dacian). . . . Love, hunger and fear are the basic factors that rule mankind, primitive or cultured ; factors uninfluenced by environment or civilization.' One instance will suffice : ' One day a guest, two days a guest, the third a nuisance ' (Urdu) ; ' Guests and fish stink on the third day ' (Montenegrin) ; ' Fresh fish and new-come guests smell in three days ' (English) ; ' After three days, a woman, a guest and the rain become very tiresome ' (Latin) ; and there are others ! Such parallelisms and similiarities are in some instances due to conquest and intermarriage ; in most, to the psychological channels and furrows of human thought.

Dr Champion's selected proverbs are given in English : he could not, logically, add originals—for thousands of originals have been lost. Such translations as I have tested are both faithful and idiomatic, but nobody is more keenly aware than the editor of the fact posited in the Italian proverb : ' Translators, traitors '. That particular proverb illustrates the potential value of a juxtaposed original, the Italian being *traddutori, traditori* ; clearly, the origin of this proverb is visual similitude. And the editor might perhaps have quoted it in full : ' Translators : traitors to the author that falls into their hands ' (*trad-dutori, traditori dell' autore che cade sotto le loro ugne*). It is not idle to note that the Italian words, *traddutori—traditori*, come from Latin words of which the first element is *trans*, ' across ', ' from one to another '.

But the truth of the proverb is in the tasting. The trouble is, there's so much to taste ! Nevertheless, here is a bill of fare, made after an agony of omission and an anguish of selection from this fascinating collection of well-tried wisdom. Before passing to a few subject-symphonies, let us hearken to a racial opus—the Bantu, culled from the original aphorisms of various tribes. ' Where you have once set your cooking-pot, throw no stones ', with which compare the English ' Don't foul your own nest ' ; ' Work is good, provided you do not forget to live ' ; ' There are forty kinds of lunacy but only one kind of common sense ' ; ' A debt is not a corpse ' ; ' The earth is a beehive ; we all enter by the same door but live in different cells ' ; ' Every beast roars in its own den ' ; ' A man who creates trouble seldom eats it himself ' ; ' To-day is to-day ! ' Against the last, offset the English ' To-morrow is a new day ', which has in the United States become ' To-morrow is also a day '. There are, as might be expected, many salutary admonitions, many urgent warnings against the folly, the danger, the spinelessness of habitual procrastination. ' He who has no will, leaves no will ; but he who leaves no will, leaves a peck of trouble.' As the Cockney said, ' Experience does it ' ; for however hard it is usually the only effectual teacher.

From the bewildering number of possibles, the following subjects have been chosen : love, wives, marriage, children, luck and destiny, character, and, for a happy ending, happiness.

' Eyes meet eyes, and love slips out between ' (Hindustani) would, to an Occidental, refer rather to fugitive ocular contacts than to permanent relations. ' Love can't be hid by hiding ', ' Love is as dust ' (that is, it must show itself), ' Love, musk, and a cough cannot be suppressed or concealed ' : all these come from India, as also do ' If there be love, impossibilities will become possible ' (the Latin *amor omnia vincit*) and ' Love alone will abide '.

Italy provides the following—and others : ' If the wife sins, the husband is not innocent ', the sin being infidelity ; nevertheless, ' Water, smoke, and a bad wife drive men out of the house ', which reminds us of the modern English ' Cigar-ash keeps the moth out and the " old

45

man " in '. ' Choose a wife and oxen from your own country ' is, in another part of Italy, ' Get your wife and your nag from a neighbour '. ' He who has had a wife deserves a crown of patience, but he who has had two deserves a strait-waistcoat ' is varied in the form, ' The first wife is matrimony, the second company, the third heresy '. All these, however, must yield in point to ' In buying horses and in taking a wife, shut your eyes tight and commend yourself to God '.

Lest this should be considered as mere Italian cynicism, I hasten to quote the English ' Honest men marry ; wise men not at all ' and ' He that marries a widow with three daughters marries four thieves '. English, too, is the sensuous ' Marry a down pillow and you have a feather bed '. And so is the profoundest of all the marriage proverbs : ' More belongs to marriage than four bare legs in a bed '.

' Fools and children speak the truth ' is a Spanish saying with parallels in other countries. ' Every child brings its own luck ', say the Germans. The Scottish declare that ' When children are young they make their parents' heads ache ; when they are old they make their hearts ache ', which in Wiltshire assumes the form, ' Children be first a yearm-ache [armache] and a'terwards a heart-ache ' ; but the Welsh express a universal truth in ' A child in the house is a hundred enjoyments ', beside which one may set the old marriage-toast, ' May all your troubles be little ones '.

Perhaps it's a matter of luck. Although ' Luck and glass soon break ', yet ' Luck is luck's mother ' (compare ' Wealth begets wealth ') ; and if it is sometimes true that ' Good luck makes one happy, bad luck great ', it is perhaps always true that ' There is no one luckier than he who thinks himself so '. Those are German proverbs ; this is Bulgarian, ' New day—new fate '. But, as the Greeks observe, ' *Character* is destiny '.

Certainly it is character which implements that proverb-to-be, ' Happiness comes from within '. ' When the bitters of adversity are exhausted, then come the sweets of happiness ' (Chinese) is inspiriting, and it was an embittered and foolish man who said : ' There are two classes of men : those who have the means to enjoy themselves but are not happy ; and those who seek happiness and find it not ' (Arabic), for only a fool consciously seeks happiness. The wise man takes happiness wherever he meets with it, or it meets with him : and there are many, many kinds to take.

(Reprinted from *John o' London's Weekly*, July 22, 1938.)

The Gentle Art of Abbreviation

As during the last war, so in this, abbreviations flourish and constantly increase in number and complexity. All the civil and combatant Services encourage—even pander to—Abbreviation ; the newspapers have long made a ' stunt ' of it, and now they are making a practice of it, and some of them won't leave well alone but must go coining their own abbreviations ; both the newspapers and the Services (to the latter, it is also a kind of free-masonry) regard it as time-saving, which often it is not, and as efficient, which it is only if you happen to know all the abbreviations employed in an article or a report or a memorandum.

Perhaps I may be allowed to quote from the Preface to *A Dictionary of Abbreviations*, which, recently completed, is now on the market. ' This dictionary is designed to help civilians and those numerous members of H.M. Forces who are not experts in abbreviation, to make their way amid that jungle of abbreviations through which news-paper readers and sailors, soldiers, airmen and Civil Defence have to thrust, like intrepid explorers, either in the search for truth or in the execution of their martial duty.

' Civilians (except Civil Servants) can afford to regard abbreviations either as a game or as an attempt (exasperat-ing though it may sometimes be) at extrication from a verbal maze, but airmen and soldiers and sailors cannot afford to regard them so light-heartedly. Petty Officers and N.C.O.s, and inexperienced officers in any of the

48

Services, regard abbreviations as something more than a joke : and even experienced officers and Warrant Officers may find themselves at a loss when confronted with a new one or when they meet with a long set of instructions issuing from a Service not their own and couched in an abbreviology that may, in their first feeling of stupefaction, strike them as uncomfortably near to demonology.'

Abbreviations are of two kinds. The first consists of abridgements, e.g. *det* for detachment ; and shortenings, e.g. *fmn* for formation.

The second consists of initials, which fall into two subclasses : separate entities, such as *F.* for Fahrenheit and *C.* for Centigrade ; and combinations, such as *A.D.C.* for aide-de-camp : it is with these that this article is concerned.

Initials in combination are either the old, well-established abbreviations of the professions, politics, science and art, such as *M.A.*, Master of Arts, and *R.A.*, Royal Academy, and *I.N.R.I.*, Jesus the Nazarene, King of the Jews ; or the new abbreviations thrown up by this war or renewed by it or thrust into prominence by it.

Let us consider only the abbreviations either created or renovated by the war of 1939–? They, after all, are a minor horror : we can take them.

They are related to civil life on the one hand and to fighting on the other. Civil life may be exemplified by the following American and English abbreviations. Very serviceable and most worthy are *A.C.*, the Atlantic Charter, preceded by *L.L.*, the Lease-Lend bill or its operations ; the American proponent is familiarly known as *F.D.R.*, whereas diplomatic courtesy, journalistic manners, and the common man's decency have forbidden the ' initialization ' of the English signatory's name. American too are *C.I.O.*, the Committee for—occasionally, Congress of—Industrial Organizations ; *A.F. of L.*, the American Federation of Labour ; *N.R.A.* (or *NRA*), the National Recovery Act—or Administration—of America, originally known only in its full form, *N.I*(ndustrial)*R.A.* ; and *U.M.W.A.*, the United Mine Workers of America. America so far has no exact equivalent of the *B.E.M.*, or British Empire Medal, and the *G.M.*, or George Medal, the civilian equivalent of the *V.C.*, though it possesses several bodies doing approximately the same work as our *R.I.I.A.*, the Royal Institute of International Affairs. The home section of the *C.S.* is known as the *H.C.S.* or Home Civil Service.

Midway between civil life and that of the combatant services is the chequered existence of Civil Defence (*C.D.*), with its *A.F.S.* or Auxiliary Fire Service, its *C.D.A.S.* or Civil Defence Ambulance Service, its *D.E.L.* or Defence Electric Light, its *P.A.D.* or Passive Air Defence, its *R.P.*, Rescue Party, and *F.A.P.* or First Aid Post, its *F.H.* or fire hydrant, often further shortened to *H.*, and, not least, its *W.R.I.* or War Risk Insurance.

Passing from the civil and defensive to the offensive, I take the three combatant services in their order of seniority. (' When in doubt, play safe ' is a bad motto for a general, a good one for a writer.)

To a civilian, *C.B.* probably evokes a Commander of the Bath ; to the Navy, almost certainly a Confidential Book (' But, hush ! we are observed ') ; let us pass over what it means to a soldier ! Other Naval abbreviations that may be listed without contravening the *O.S.A.* (Official Secrets Act) are *C.N.S.* and *C.N.P.*, respectively the First Sea Lord and the Second Sea Lord ' in their official capacities ' of Chief of the Naval Staff and Chief

of Naval Personnel ; *F.D.O.* and *F.E.O.* are those differently useful persons, the Fleet Dental Officer and the Fleet
Engineer Officer. Clear to the Navy but probably very
obscure to civilians are three other officers, in occasional
rather than permanent roles : the *O.O.G.*, the *O.O.Q.*,
and the *O.O.W.*, who, in plain English, are respectively
the Officer of the Guard, the Officer of the Quarters, and
the Officer of the Watch. The *R.N.* must not be forgotten
in its offshoots the *R.N.R.*, the Royal Navy Reserve, and
the *R.N.V.R.*, the Royal Navy Volunteer Reserve.

At the head of the Army is the *G.O.C.-in-C.* or General
Officer Commanding-in-Chief (i.e., at its head) ; any
further initials, or any docking of initials, would imply
that he isn't ! For instance, the *C.-in-C. H.F.* is the
Commander-in-Chief of the Home Forces, and the *G.O.C.-
in-C. M.E.* is the General at the head of our forces in the
Middle East. ('The Near East' has joined Atlantis in
the limbo of geographical discards.) Other Army officers
and ranks worthy of abbreviated notice are the various
Directors, such as the *D.A.P.S.*, Director of Army Postal
Services ; *D.M.S.*, Medical Services ; *D.A.E.*, Army
Education (*A.E.*, not to be confused with *AE*, indicating
a ship that is third-class in Lloyd's Register) ; and the
various Deputies of this or that, such as the *D.A.G.* or
Deputy Adjutant-General, and *their* deputies (' . . . and so
ad infinitum '), the Deputy Assistants—*D.A.A.G.*, the
Deputy Assistant Adjutant-General, the *D.A.D.M.S.*, the
Deputy Assistant Director of Medical Services, the
D.A.Q.M.G., Deputy Assistant Quartermaster General,
who, in *Q*, corresponds to the *D.A.A.G.* in *A*, *Q* being the
Quartermaster's branch, *A* the Adjutant's (postings, per-
sonnel, crimes, leave, welfare). The G.S.O.s or General
Staff Officers are of three grades, referred to more briefly

as *G.1*, *G.2*, and *G.3*, the last group being the (admittedly rather superior) ' dog's bodies ' of a Divisional, Corps, Command, or Army headquarters (*H.Q.*) staff. These and other officers of the Army have frequent recourse to three ' books of words '—*F.S.R.*, Field Service Regulations ; *F.S.P.B.*, the Field Service Pocket Book, which—the most exciting of the three—appears in serial form ; and, above all, *K.R.*, ' King's Regs ', The King's Regulations for the Army and the Army Reserve, which, to commit the unforgivable sin of self-quotation, is ' the Bible of the officer, the God of the sergeant-major (especially Warrant Officers, Class I), and the sure shield of the knowledgeable private '.

The *R.F.C.*, Royal Flying Corps, of the last war, has long been the *R.A.F.*, with its offshoots the *R.A.F.V.R.*, the Royal Air Force Volunteer Reserve (often shortened to *V.R.*) and the *R.A.F.O.* or Reserve of Air Force Officers. Whereas *B.C.* is Bomber Command, *F.C.* is Fighter Command and *C.C.* is Coastal Command. Some of the other Allied air forces are the *R.A.A.F.*, Australian ; *R.C.A.F.*, Canadian ; *R.S.A.A.F.*, South African ; *A.V.G.*, the already famous American Volunteer Group of airmen ' star '-spangling China and Burma and not forming part of the *U.S.A.C.* or United States Air Corps.

Of those abbreviations which are common to the three fighting Services, several that have different meanings are worth noting. In the Navy and the Air Force, *E.O.* denotes Engineer Officer, but in the Army it denotes Education Officer or, improperly, Entertainments Officer (*Ents O.*). To the Navy, *F.O.* means Flag Officer ; to the Army, Field Officer ; to the Air Force, Flying Officer ; Civil Servants, however, would immediately think of the Foreign Office. To the Air Force, *T.B.* is a torpedo bomber, to the Navy a torpedo boat, to the Army a training battalion.

In the words of the Other Ranks of the Army, ' what a game it is ! ' Nevertheless, an expert knowledge of abbreviations is an Open Sesame to many official doors and ' that blessed word *Mesopotamia* ' to many official minds. By their abbreviations shall ye know them !

(John o' London's Weekly, May 1942.)

Those Radio Catch-phrases

A.—*Well, I know, of course, what radio is, but to be honest, I'm not quite sure whether a catch-phrase is the same as a commonplace or whether there's some tricky distinction between the two things.*

B.—*A distinction ; but not tricky. Examples, however, are better than definitions.* (Hesitates.)

A.—*Yes ?*

B.—*Examples of clichés—commonplaces to you—are the politicians' ' to explore every avenue ' and melodrama's ' a fate worse than death '. And examples of catch-phrases are ' Does your mother know you're out ? ', ' Sez you ! ', ' Well, what do you know ! ', and ' What would you do, chums ? '*

A.—*' What would you do, chums ? ' It was Syd Walker who said that, wasn't it ?*

B.—*It was. But please allow me . . .*

SYD WALKER, the far from dusty philosopher, who most untimely died during ' the recent spot of bother ', was, as millions of listeners will remember, the tonic star of the pre-war radio programme, *Band Waggon*. He used to propound the quaintest problems and ask, ' What would you do, chums ? ' The phrase ' caught on ' : became a catch-phrase. I should be a rich man if I had a pound for every time I heard that phrase in the Army and the R.A.F. during the years 1940–45.

Yet, popular though Syd Walker's humorous query was, there is one that has had an even wider currency. In 1939, two important things happened. The war and *Itma*. I don't know who thought of that title for a radio programme. Maybe it was the irrepressible Tommy Handley himself. Or his brilliant scriptwriter. Anyway, ' It's that man again ' was, during the bombing of Britain in 1940–41 and, sporadically, later, often heard, sometimes with an incarnadined epithet preceding ' man ', in relation to bomb-damage, whether a church demolished, a ' local ' closed or a gas-supply temporarily out of action ; rather like ' the mice have been at it ', itself a reminiscence of a very famous Bruce Bairnsfather cartoon of the 1914–18 war. And since the more recent war, even so late as just the other day, I have often heard the phrase. Any constant caller is apt to announce himself with ' It's (or ' It's only ') that man again '.

Other *Itma* phrases that have gained a public currency are the ' Can I do you now, sir ? ' of Mrs Mopp (Dorothy Summers) ; ' After you, Claude—No, after you, Cecil ' ; ' I don't mind if I do ' ; ' Boss, something terrible's happened ', in Sam Scram's comically tragic tones. But it would be tedious to enumerate all the catch-phrases originated by *Itma*.

Band Waggon has, besides ' What would you do, chums ? ', given us at least two phrases, both of them spoken by Arthur Askey : ' Hullo, playmates ! ' and ' I thenk you ! ' The latter phrase would have had a longer life if it had not been for the difficulty people experienced in trying to imitate Arthur Askey's inimitable intonation.

Merry-Go-Round appeared during the war in three versions—the Army's, the Navy's, the Air Force's. From one or other of these come ' Read any good books lately ? ' (the Horne-Murdoch opening gambit), ' Hush, keep it dark ' (from the mouth of Commander High-Price), and, by far the most famous of them, ' Steady, Barker ! ' which, from the Naval version, has often been successfully employed by those who wished to steady themselves, or others, with a terse equivalent of ' Pull your socks up, old man ! ' or ' Get a grip on yourself, old girl ! ' ' Steady, Barker ! ' is also the most interesting of the *Merry-Go-Round* phrases, for it is the Naval re-shaping of the Army's (hence of many civilians') very old catch-phrase : ' Steady, the Buffs ! ' which was born of an anecdote told of, and by, that long-established and distinguished regiment which, from about 1740, was, after its buff-coloured facings and the name of its 1737–49 commanding officer, called ' the Buff Howards ', shortened in the 19th century (and afterwards) to ' the Buffs '.

From *Stand Easy*, a post-war version of *Merry-Go-Round*, comes, ' I say, what a smasher ! ' which crystallizes and renders articulate the semi-articulate *smasher*, an attractive girl (or man), a fine aircraft, an excellent ' what-have-you ', and its corresponding adjective *smashing*, as in ' I say, what a smashing piece of homework ! ' As an approbatory adjective, *smashing* has, in the Armed Forces (and since 1944 among civilians), been near-rivalled only by *lush*, short for ' luscious ' ; in the Navy, indeed, *lush* was more widely used than *smashing*. With *smasher*, compare its predecessors ' lady-*killer* ' and ' *breaker* of men's hearts '—terms that, in the language of philologists, constitute the semantic origin of *smasher*.

In providing us with so many substitutes for thought (although they are also much more than that), the radio programmes have followed the breezy, cheerful example of the music-hall and the Variety theatre, which have either originated or helped to popularize a number of catch-phrases, several of which have almost become proverbs. As, for instance, Marie Lloyd's ' A little of what you fancy does you good ', with several variations ; ' Everything in the garden's lovely ', said to have been coined by Royalty but certainly taken up by the music-halls ; and ' How's your poor feet ? '

More than radio, more than music-hall, ' all the world and his wife ' (or his girl) have started the catch-phrase on its leaping, laughing career. A career often started by the genius of a dramatist or a novelist. Dickens, for instance, provided us with several, the best known being perhaps ' Barkis is willing '—from his best-known book, *David Copperfield*.

Yet there is something very noticeable about radio-programme phrases. They seem, most of them, to have a very short life. Remember, however, that the radio programme of the kind that can yield such phrases is a comparatively recent force in entertainment. Remember, too, that the very multiplicity of these radio catch-phrases works against them ; the competition is too hot ; all the weaklings fall by the fireside.

But *why* does any phrase emerge ? Because it is happily topical ; or because it has a catchy phrasing ; or because it is self-preserved with the salt of humour ; or because, in rare instances, it implies—never preaches—an invigorating message or motto, indicative of courage without cant or of philosophical point without priggishness, and sprung from the invincible fortitude of the average Britisher.

Psychologically, a catch-phrase often plays the part of a cigarette or a pipe in times of fear or nervousness, in periods of stress or distress. In a world momentarily or temporarily strange or bewildering or hostile or dangerous it serves the ordinary person, you and me and the other fellow, much as a floating spar does a shipwrecked mariner or as, to a lonely traveller, a known face glimpsed in a foreign land. Amid the unfamiliar it is familiar ; it is

57

something to grasp and to hold. Its triviality is transcended. Perhaps, rather, its very triviality is helpful, comforting, heartening.

(Written in November, and published in
The Radio Times on December 6, 1946.)

Japanese Intruders

IN the 19th century, it was usual to regard Japan (all peoples except the British call it Nippon) as the modern Oriental equivalent of feudal Europe : quaint, full of the most charmingly homely virtues, chivalrous, artistic, deeply religious. During the Russo-Japanese War and for some years after it, the Japanese were extolled as the collective embodiment of all the heroic virtues, and *the brave little Japs* went near to becoming a cliché. After about 1920, their stock lowered ; they were, obviously, poking their noses into everything (universities, science, industry, armament), and many intelligent persons began to suspect their suave insincerity and their diplomatic evasions.

In view of the facile glamour attaching to Japan and the Japanese, the number of Japanisms adopted into English, even among the educated and the cultured, is surprisingly small : some seventeen native Japanese words and several anglicizations of Japanese words or phrases ; and of those seventeen only five appeared in W. W. Skeat's *An Etymological Dictionary of the English Language* (4th edition, 1910), although fourteen occurred in Ernest Weekley's *An Etymological Dictionary of Modern English* (1921). Weekley is much the more alert linguistic observer.

Among the earliest words to be adopted were *japan*, *Mikado*, *jinriksha*, *soy*, *hara-kiri*, *Shinto*.

The noun and verb, *japan*, patently derive from the name of the country, and the noun is the earlier ; it represents an ellipsis of *Japan work*. Pope, in *The Rape of*

59

the Lock, jocosely refers to 'shining altars of Japan'. The verb means 'to varnish (something) as Japan work is varnished', hence little more than 'to polish' (compare the playful *japanner*, 'a shoe-black', likewise in Pope).

The Mikado, so long a mythical and aweful figure, now a figure of seclusive pathos, became almost 'a household word' when Gilbert and Sullivan used it for the title of one of the three best of their musical comedies. The Emperor of Japan's title comes from *mikado*, 'high gate' : *mi*, 'exalted', and *kado*, 'a gate, a door'. *Mikado*, therefore, provides an interesting racial comparison with the Turkish *Sublime Porte* ; for the Turkish Government, as Webster's International informs us, is 'officially called the Sublime Porte, from the *port* (gate) of the sultan's palace, where justice was administered'. *Sublime Porte* is a reversal —a perversion—of the French *porte sublime*, which translates *Babi Ali* (literally, 'the high gate'). *Bab* occurs also in Arabic, as in Bab el Mandeb, the gateway to the Red Sea ; so does *ali* or *aliy*.

From the sublime to the serviceable. Originally the grandees, but latterly all those persons who can afford one, have in Japan been conveyed in the jinriksha or hooded, two-wheeled, man-drawn carriage, which, nowadays, is usually called *rickshaw*, so well known in other Oriental countries ; in India, the jinriksha used to be named *Jennyrickshaw*, by that particular process of folklore which is termed 'Hobson-Jobson'. The word *jinriksha* consists of three elements (properly they are radicals) : *jin*, 'a man' ; *riki*, 'strength' ; *sha*, 'a carriage' : clearly, therefore, it is in fact what it is in etymology, 'a car drawn by strength of man'. The comparative philologist may detect cognates or perhaps merely delusive similarities with Hindustani or other Asiatic-Indian words ; but such slippery ground is not for us.

Indian sauces are more famous than Japanese, yet *soy* was known to Englishmen as early as the 1690's : Dampier, in *A New Voyage*, speaks of ' Japan, from whence the true *soy* comes '. *The English Cyclopaedia* tells us that the Japanese prepare, with the seeds of the Dolichos soja, a variety of bean, the sauce called *sooja*, which name has, in English, taken the form *soy*. Strictly, the word is *shoyu* ; and *shoyu* is the sauce made from the *daidzu* bean. It is instructive to note that we now speak of ' soya beans ' ; the form *soya* indicates a Dutch influence. Oriental words suffer the strangest mutations when they are exposed to the alchemy of English !

From beans to hara-kiri may be a shorter, more natural step than might at first seem probable. Ceremonial hara-kiri is *seppuku* ; unceremonious suicides and battlefield suicides, except by aristocrats and generals, would be called *hara-kiri*, which means, literally, ' suicide by disembowelment ', or, by division into elements, *hara*, ' belly ', and *kiri*, ' to cut '. The alternate ' happy dispatch ', now obsolescent, affords another example of Hobson-Jobson.

Shinto, the national religion of the Japanese, permits seppuku and hara-kiri. *Shinto* derives, as so many Japanese cultural words do, from the Chinese : *shin tao*, ' way of the gods ' ; with *way*, compare the use of the word in the New Testament.

We may now pass to more modern terms ; that is, more modern as adoptions by the English language. The hereditary commander of the Japanese army is domestically the Shogun, externally the Tycoon. Both *Shogun*, ' chief ', and *Tycoon*, ' mighty prince ', come from the

Chinese, and the latter term has passed into the American language with the senses 'big chief', 'big shot', 'magnate'.

Daimio is an obsolete title for a great nobleman. Literally 'great name' (compare 'the great names of history'), it has been adopted from Chinese. 'In the good old days', a Samurai was a member of the military caste ; he stood in much the same relationship to a Daimio as that in which, in medieval England, an esquire stood to a knight. In modern Japan, a Samurai is an army officer but not, of course, a mere 'temporary gentleman'. In his *The New Utopia*, Mr H. G. Wells used the word—the same in the plural as in the singular, be it noted—for ' the bosses', whom he had previously called 'New Republicans'; the latter term had been still-born. A *two-sworded man*, according to a knowledgeable friend of the writer's, is ' rather a swell brand of daimio. I've known one, but can't say I was impressed by feudal grandeur.' A *Ronin*, literally 'wave man', is applied to one of gentle blood who, having become separated from his feudal lord, wanders about the country as a somewhat disreputable knight-errant ; the term came to denote a hired bravo, or even a bandit neither pure nor simple.

Bushido is rather the national code of honour than the code of national honour. The aforementioned 'knowledgeable' writes thus :—' Apparently a damned fake invented for European consumption at the time of the Russo-Japanese War. So far as I can ascertain, it never existed in the Japanese language before the present century, but for propaganda purposes it has been disseminated as if it came down from the feudal times.'

Bushido throws an interesting light, though less interesting than that shed by the Japanese parleys in Washington on the eve of Pearl Harbour, on the Japanese use of *honourable*, as in ' honourable ancestors ' ; the word now tends to have an ironic tinge. Another Japanism is *elder statesman*, which we adopted rather less than a generation ago and which we applied to Balfour and to Lloyd George once they had ceased to be violently active but while they retained some considerable faculty of delivering advice from on high.

Banzai, the Japanese war-cry (literally ' ten thousand years ' : cf. the Chinese *wan*, ' myriad ', and *sui*, ' year '), has, in England, become apprehended as ' hurrah ! ' It occurs, for instance, in *Toikoku banzai !*, ' long live the Empire ! ' During the war of 1939–1945, it has been much less heard of than it was during the Russo-Japanese unpleasantness. Even *jiu-jitsu* seems to have lost much of its magic : a well-trained British or Canadian commando would probably reduce an average jiu-jitsuist to impotence before the latter could establish an unbreakable hold. More correctly *ju-jutsu*, the term means ' muscle-science '.

But geisha girls will doubtless charm many hot-blooded American and British soldiers. Literally, *geisha* signifies no more than ' dancing-girl ' ; the English notion of the word is less charitable, for it implies a somewhat uneasy virtue and a not intransigent chastity. Many such girls and many more that are, frankly, entirely commercial, live in the Yoshiwara or ' flower districts ' : ' A pretty girl is like a flower '. In that district—as, however, in many reputable ones also—much *saké* is consumed. This fermented liquor, made from rice, is popularly supposed, in Britain, to be exceedingly potent ; ' but I must say ' (thus the valuable, valued correspondent already quoted) ' from personal experience of being a Jap's guest, it never phased me '.

63

There are a few other terms, it is true. Nevertheless, the above-mentioned words and phrases do represent an equitable selection, which includes the four best known words of all (*Mikado, hara-kiri, jiu-jitsu, geisha*) : whence it appears that the Second World War has not grafted any new Japanese terms upon the English language. Which is no great loss.

(Written in September 1945. My 1945 Christmas card.)

*Words in Vogue: Words of Power**

WORDS are very important things ; at the lowest estimate, they are indispensable counters of communication.

Words are as beacons to lighten the darkness of our ignorance, but too many of us have been blinded with an excess of light ; the excess is ours. Words are a solvent of clotted prejudice, but too many of us have made of them a reinforcement of the insensate atavism of inherited opinions. We have allowed too many of the beacons to become wreckers' lights ; too many of them to become self-important and arrogantly autonomous. Especially during a war. We saw their importance exaggerated in 1914–18, when to say *Hun* was to knock your opponent insensible with an unanswerable bludgeon. In the interval between the two great wars, *Bolshie*—though less in the

---

* As this is not a lexicographical study, I have not noted the earliest appearances of the words (or the relevant senses). For the sake of convenience, I have drawn the majority of the quotations from six notable books, chosen *after* I had formed my list, books cited illustratively with no unfavourable implication (vogue words, after all, indicate vogue—or prevalent and predominant—ideas) ; of these only one, *Strangers*, is a novel :

W. R. Inge : *Outspoken Essays*, 1919 ; 2nd series, 1922.
A. N. Whitehead : *Adventures of Ideas*, 1933.
Viscount Samuel : *Belief and Action*, 1937.
Claude Houghton : *Strangers*, 1938.
W. Theimer : *The Penguin Political Dictionary*, 1939.
Olaf Stapledon : *Beyond the Isms*, 1942—the most stimulating of them
   all.

1930's—was even more deadly. And in this war, such words as *Aryan, totalitarian, Blitzkrieg,* and such catch-phrases as *time is on our side* and *we can take it,* have become dangerously symbolic, powerful and soporific : we forget that *Aryan* merely cloaks a myth, that the only adequate reply to *totalitarian* is *total warfare,* that we should cease to regard ourselves as the heroes of the 1940–41 aerial *Blitzkrieg,* that although *time is on our side* we have turned it to poor account and time will still be on our side when we're dead, and that instead of being so masochistically eager to *take it* we might be more energetic in *giving it.*

War, however, heightens the effect of all words and phrases that possess, or seem to possess, an extrinsic power in addition to an intrinsic magic : and war makes, of fashionable words that would in peace-time die a natural and unmourned death, words of power : verbal sticks with which to beat the public or verbal drugs with which to send them to sleep,—although far too many persons are administering the drugs to themselves and thereby committing spiritual hara-kiri.

With the precaution that some of the words here treated might have been classified otherwise without harming anybody (except perhaps myself) I have divided these vogue-words into four groups : Journalistic and Political ; Psychological and Philosophical ; Cultural ; and General.

First the predominantly journalistic sub-group, into which many of the political words and phrases, and a few words from the second and third groups might have been put : life cannot be watertight-compartmented as impermeably as many writers on language would like, *tant pis pour eux !*

Bid has become extremely fashionable among journalists for a very simple and potent reason : this noun is so

very much shorter than ' attempt ', ' endeavour ', ' enter-
prise ', although it is of the same length as ' aim ', which
it also, and most unnecessarily, displaces. This ' rubber-
stamp word ', as Mr Frank Whitaker wittily described it
a few years ago, is a convenience in headlines ; as though
mere typographical convenience were everything ! ' Here
they '—the German army—' are making a determined
bid to move on Acroma and cut the main road linking
Tobruk to Gazala ' is a sentence in *The Sunday Express*,
June 14, 1942 : but it is somewhat startling to find Dean
Inge speaking of ' a bid for the popular vote ' (*Outspoken
Essays*, 1919), even though its use is there almost justifiable.

The shape of things to come and *brave new world* have
literary origins, their immediate popularity arising from
the famous works of Mr H. G. Wells and Mr Aldous
Huxley ; both of these phrases, however, are rather
clichés than powerful vogues. Wholly relevant is *Blitzkrieg*
(lightning war), which has even found a place in the
January 1942 edition of Walter Theimer's invaluable
Political Dictionary ; the chief derivative is *blitz*, noun and
verb. Another German term is *ersatz*, ' substitute ', a
revival from the war of 1914–18.

Much more frequently used in the two years preceding,
and during, this war than in 1914–18 : *crisis*. The Munich
Agreement (' the peace that passeth all understanding ',
as a disgusted journalist described it at the time) was but
the first of many *crises* : so much so that we should feel
uncomfortable if we had not to face at least a serious crisis
and preferably a tautologically *grave crisis*.

The definitely political group—that is, words and
phrases that, however much used by journalists, remain
predominantly political—is much larger ; it forms an
interesting and important list : *economic* (*man*, etc.) ;

bourgeois, Communism (and *proletariat*), *democracy, Naziism* and *Fascism, dictatorship ; New Order, power politics, Herren-volk, Führerprinzip, Lebensraum, corporate state, totalitarian, total war(fare) ; scrap of paper, sanctions, appeasement ; Aryan, militarist, barbarism ;* and *integration*.

Dean Inge, 1919, mentions that ' unreal abstraction—the " economic man " ', a relic of Victorian economics. Professor A. N. Whitehead, in 1933, says, ' We can all remember our old friend, the economic man. The beauty of the economic man was that we knew exactly what he was after. Whatever his wants were, he knew them and his neighbours knew them ' (*Adventures of Ideas*). But *economic* figures also in the following oft-recurring phrases : *economic interpretation of history* (Whitehead), *economic factor, economic conditions, economic necessity,* and *economic system* : several of them occur notably, for example, in Viscount Samuel's *Belief and Action,* 1937.

Bourgeois and *bourgeoisie* have, among Socialists and Communists, ousted ' middle-class ' and ' the middle-class ' ; mostly because of Marx, who applied *bourgeoisie* to ' the class of proprietors (other than agricultural), capitalists, manufacturers, merchants, persons with a business of their own, leading employees and members of liberal professions equal to them in income, education and social standing, as opposed to the " proletariat " ' (Theimer). In Mr Claude Houghton's *Strangers,* 1938, we find one of the characters asserting that ' [Mediocrity's] the god of the bourgeois '.—Here it may be interpolated that this sensitive and spiritually alert man of letters is extremely valuable to any systematic investigator of vogue words, words of national import ; particularly his *Hudson Rejoins the Herd* and *Strangers*.—Not that the bourgeois need worry about the label. Mr Olaf Stapledon, in his profound and brilliant *Beyond the Isms*, 1942, has noted that 'like Puritanism, science was made possible by the rise of the bourgeois '.

Proletariat is a convenient—though to some a derogatory —term for the working classes, especially if we remember that many middle-class people work harder than the vast majority of the working classes. 'The introduction of machinery, the gathering together of masses of workers, an unrestrained competition in the labour-market, together with recurring cycles of bad trade, created the modern proletariat and brought untold numbers into misery ', as Viscount Samuel has said in *Belief and Action*, where the term is often used. It occurs also in the already quoted works of Houghton, Stapledon, and Theimer, who notes that *proletariat* strictly applies to property-less wage-earners. *Communism* and *Communist* do not require exemplification.

But something should be said of *democracy* and *democratic*. Since he now thinks rather differently, it is perhaps hardly fair to quote Dean Inge's criticism (*Outspoken Essays*) ; yet I do so, because *democracy*, despite its failings, now stands in unhappily heightened relief. 'The doctrinaire democrat still '—in 1919—' vapours about democracy, though representative government has obviously lost both its power and its prestige.' Professor Whitehead has written, ' In the last quarter of the eighteenth century, Democracy was born, with its earliest incarnations in America and in France ' (1933). Mr Theimer has expressed what is the sad recognition by many of us that ' democracy has been challenged by " authoritarian " tendencies in recent times, and dictatorships, denying democratic methods and rights, have sprung up in a number of countries ', and, a year earlier, Viscount

Samuel made some arresting references to this theme in *Belief and Action*.

Naziism (now generally *Nazism*) and *Fascism*, with the adjectives *Nazi* and *Fascist* are almost too much with us to make quotation necessary. Theimer's articles on these allied political creeds are worth re-reading for their sound commonsense, but Olaf Stapledon's paragraphs attain to that much higher sphere of *good* sense and penetrating insight, as when (in 1942) he says that ' Nazism is the *reductio ad absurdum* of pure collectivism ; but it is also, I believe, an obscure protest against materialism, a tragically confused and perverted reassertion of the " spirit " ', or when, of the 1920's and early 1930's, he says that ' there was a longing for a new and bracing idea to save man from his directionless, self-indulgent way of living. This was the social situation which bred the exasperated, neurotic condition favourable to Fascism and Nazism.' Notable, too, is the long chapter on ' What Fascism Is ', in Professor Laski's *Where Do We Go From Here?* (1940).

Dictatorship, although it has already been mentioned, does merit further mention. In 1937, with what now seems like prophetic foresight, Viscount Samuel wrote, ' Dictatorships, it must be agreed, have their advantages, at all events at the outset. There may be speed of action and efficiency of administration such as democracies sometimes lack.' A year later, Claude Houghton penetratingly remarked, ' Dictators yelled that they represented a united nation, but, actually, dictatorship was only the recognition of a permanent state of civil war '. It was above all, dictator Hitler who had spoken so glibly and delusively of *the New Order* ; Italy and Japan have parroted this Germanic cry. Its origin is implicatively seen in Viscount Samuel's lament, uttered in 1937. ' Nor is there any clear vision anywhere of new ideas for the founding of a new order '—' of a beneficent kind ', he should have added.

Intimate constituents of the *Herrenvolk's* New Order are the doctrines of *Führerprinzip* and *Lebensraum*. Stapledon records two ' causes of Nazism . . . peculiar to Germany ' : traditional ' opposition to the civilization of Western Europe ' and ' the fact that this great people with its recurrent dream of becoming the acknowledged " Herrenvolk " [master-people] of the world, had suffered a decisive defeat in war '. On June 22, 1942, *The Daily Telegraph*, in a leader, has the biting sentence, ' Confident boasts that Russia would be beaten in three months . . . and the Herrenvolk subdue the Slavs for ever have vanished behind the shadows of millions of German dead and wounded '.

Even Herrenvolk require a leader ; that the Germans, the most mass-suggestible nation in the world, not merely require but welcome a fiery, autocratic leader must be obvious to all except the most indurated of wishful-thinkers. Of the *Führerprinzip* (literally, leader-principle), as on so many other things, Viscount Samuel has a trenchant remark. ' The Fascist-Nazi system is based upon another doctrine, besides internationalism, militarism and the Hegelian conception of the State—the principle of personal leadership. The aura surrounding the State is extended to the spokesman. Here the new philosophy pursues earlier tendencies. Frequently recurring in both German and Italian history is the cult of the Hero. The present *Führerprinzip* is the formulation of old practice.'

Even more notorious is the doctrine of *Lebensraum*,

living room or living space : ' a new slogan of German imperialism ' is Theimer's comment ; rather is it a new name for the ' place in the sun ' (*place au soleil*) of the first score years of this troubled century. It is, in practice, a flimsy excuse for unprovoked aggression (*ôte-toi de là que je m'y mette !*). So well known has *living room*, its prevalent English translation, become that *The Evening News* of July 2, 1942, could publish a Gittins cartoon representing Hitler gazing at the graves of German soldiers killed at Sebastopol and saying ' And I promised them living, room '.

Less known than *Lebensraum* but rather better known than *Führerprinzip* is *Machtpolitik* in its English form : *power politics* : a mirage-presentment of the cynically Germanic axiom that ' might is right '.

Worthy in origin but perverted in practice is *corporate state*. A corporate state might conceivably—it would be unwise to say ' probably '—be a success, although its basic principle is indubitably inferior to that of democracy. ' A practical test has not been made so far, as the corporate systems which have been set up hitherto have all been working under a dictatorship, and are little short of a pliant mask for autocracy ', as Walter Theimer has acutely noted. Nazi Germany and Fascist Italy are nominally corporate states ; in effect they are authoritarian or, rather, that exaggeratedly dictatorial form : *totalitarian* states. This ' Aryan, *-arian* ' adjective was esteemed to be worth its place in the 1934 Supplement of *The Concise Oxford Dictionary*. The definition runs : ' Relating to a polity that permits no rival royalties or parties. *T. state* (with only one, the governing, party) '. The individual is subordinated to the state ; the State is all—or almost all. There is, of course, the Führer or the Duce. ' Devotion to a man ', General Wavell remarks in *Generals and General-ship* (a series of three lectures delivered early in 1939), ' has sometimes inspired soldiers in the past. Will it do so again in the totalitarian countries ? ' Well, we know the answer to that one ! The derivative noun, *totalitarianism*, is much rarer than its parent ; it does, however, occur at least twice in Olaf Stapledon's book.

A totalitarian state is well equipped and far from reluctant to wage *total war* ; to a Hitler, any alternative to total warfare is unthinkable, and we have, since September 1939, had almost sufficient opportunity to realize the importance of total or, as we English prefer to say, ' all-out ' effort. One totalitarian state has, ever since 1914, guffawed at the validity of a *scrap of paper* ; the cogency of *sanctions* has, for some years, been sneered at by another such state ; and both of these totalitarians have, since the rape of Czechoslovakia, made a Germanic gibe and a Roman ribaldry of *appeasement*. As Viscount Samuel has mildly said, the war of 1914–18 proved that ' under stress, treaties may become mere " scraps of paper " ' : Bethmann-Hollweg's phrase, referring to the treaty guaranteeing Belgian neutrality and spoken to the British Ambassador in Berlin on August the fourth, 1918, has done Germany no good : unfortunately too many of us too soon forgot that that unethical gesture was typical of German political and military thinking.

' Sanctions and appeasement, forsooth ! ' *Sanction(s)* is a slightly puzzling word, for it has two senses that are antithetic, ' reward ' and ' punishment, penalty ' ; one neutral sense, ' authority, (official) permission ' (' The theory of democracy—*vox populi vox dei*—is a pure super-stition, a belief in a divine or natural sanction which does not exist ', Inge) ; and a further sense, a specialization

73

of the ' penalty ' one. This last is the short form of the
fuller *punitive* (or *vindicatory*) *sanction* ; is predominantly
political ; and has, in the main, resulted from the League
of Nation's usage, *sanctions* being either those penalties
which, set forth in a treaty or agreement, attach to dis-
obedience, or the statutory enforcements of those penalties.
This, now the prevalent sense, is exemplified in the cited
works of Samuel, Theimer, and Stapledon—and in scores
of others.

Appeasement, that fatuous sop to a Caesar-Cerberus and a
hungry Hitler, was assiduously practised by Britain in
1937–early 1939 ; but even Neville Chamberlain at last
perceived that this pouring of international kindness and
accommodation down a drain was an ' expense of spirit
in a waste of shame ' ; so ended the ' appeasement of
international brigandage ' (Stapledon).

Appeasement was doomed to fail against *Aryan militarist
barbarism* and against a Mussolini fortified with the com-
fortable knowledge of a Hitler backing him up. What
' that blessed word *Mesopotamia* ' was to the dear old lady
of the fable, *Aryan* has, throughout the 20th century (for
it is no new thing), been to the Germans. During the war
of 1914–18, Dean Inge could write with superb irony,
' Wherever we find marked energy and nobleness of
character, we may suspect Aryan blood ; and history will
usually support our surmise '. The Aryans were invented
by philologist Max Müller, who later recognized his error
and vigorously retracted it : ' He emphasised that
" Aryan " was only a philological term, and meant
neither blood nor bones, nor hair, nor skull. As a matter
of fact, there is no such thing as an Aryan in Europe. The
myth, however, has survived its creator and become the
principal weapon of anti-Semitism ' (Theimer). As a

74

synonym of 'non-Jewish', it is superfluous ; as a synonym of 'German', it is farcical.

Militarism and *militarist* have the merit of usefulness ; *militarist* signifies something more precise than 'warlike' on the one hand ; on the other, than 'belligerent' : as applied to Germany it denotes 'dominated by military ideas' and connotes 'having ambitions of conquest by means of a professional army'. In 1917, in an article republished in *Outspoken Essays*, Dean Inge caustically declared that 'the immunity from militarism hitherto enjoyed by Britain and the United States was a fortunate accident, not a proof of higher morality'. 'The militarist philosophy' (Samuel) of Germany had its roots in the Dark Ages ; it was revived, in practice, by Frederick the Great ; it was lyricized by Nietzsche and systematized by Treitschke ; and Hitler has apotheosized it.

Barbarians and *barbarism* were terms frequently applied to the Germans in the war of 1914–18 : and they have been resuscitated and refurbished for use in this war. That Professor Whitehead was, even in 1933, distrustful of the Germans is clear from the following brief passages from *Adventures of Ideas*. 'Barbarism and civilization were at odds with each other, and we stand for civilization.' —'A Barbarian speaks in terms of power. He dreams of the superman with the mailed fist. He may plaster his lust with sentimental morality of Carlyle's type. But ultimately his final good is conceived as one will imposing itself upon other wills. This is intellectual barbarism.' No journalist has put the case so cogently ; no man of letters so tersely.

Against barbarism, kid gloves are ineffectual. As a factor of democratic aggressiveness, however, co-ordination has its value. That brings us to what is the latest vogue-word. *Integration.* ' Integration of personality ' has for some years been a commonplace among psychologists, in politics it is new. From *The Daily Telegraph* of June 29, 1942, comes this paragraph over the name of that witty composite ' Peterborough ' (a sort of Siamese sextet) :— ' After a noteworthy career of some seven years the word " co-ordination " is fast becoming demoded in the best political quarters. Any M.P. who wants to keep abreast of the times is now careful to speak of " integration ". So much is the word to the fore in Ministerial statements and Whitehall announcements that I suspect a co-ordinated—I mean integrated—move to secure its adoption. It has obvious advantages. It saves a hyphen, to say nothing of a letter.'

As psychology has ' lost ' *integration,* so it has given a number of terms to become vogue words. From psychology and the other philosophies have come the following, a number of which might equally well be considered in the next—the Cultural—group. These are *organism* ; *atavistic, ideology, moral anarchy, code* ; to *condition* ; *the ego* ; *neurosis* and *psychosis, repression, inhibition, sublimation, complex* and *wishful thinking* ; *space-time* and *cosmos* (and *cosmic process*) ; *scientific attitude* ; *individualist* and *self-expression* (or *-realization*) ; *spiritual values.*

Organism, a scientific term, has been much used in the political sciences and in the philosophies. As Viscount Samuel has said, ' We may be misled by a metaphor or an analogy. The State in some respects resembles an organism. . . . But the State is not in fact an organism. That is a biological term, and the State is not biological.' Some fifteen years earlier, Dean Inge had suggested that ' the " social organism " is a very low type of organism '. Spengler, who, perhaps deliberately, confused many issues, gave it as his opinion that ' cultures are organisms, and world history is their collective biography ' ; but *Kultur* bears too many marks of being a regimented organization.

To such an organization, with its *ideology* and its *moral anarchy*, we must oppose a genuine *code* of faith and fortitude. The ideology has much of the *atavistic*. ' Pugnacity, greed, mere excitement, the contagion of a crowd . . . are plainly atavistic and pathological ' (Inge). Much newer than *atavistic* is *ideology*, which originally meant the science of ideas but has also come to mean visionary speculations and, especially in reference to Germany and Italy, a system of political ideas subserving a national aim (world-dominion ; imperial Rome). We can speak, too, of ' the Marxian ideology ' (Stapledon).

One set of ideologies may—and often does—speak of its ideological opponents as exponents of *moral anarchy*, which often follows on that intellectual barbarism to which Whitehead alluded. A good example of the phrase occurs in this ironically rhetorical question, ' Shall we say : It is liberty of thought and action which has brought these confusions ; let us abandon liberty ; let us follow whoever has the courage to seize power and the cunning to control ideas ; let us accept intellectual tyranny for fear of moral anarchy ? ' (Samuel, 1937).

To moral anarchy, moralists would oppose a moral *code* : prudence hints that we should also enlist an intellectual code and a spiritual code. Whitehead points out that ' the codes of all religions also embody the particular temperaments and stages of civilization of their adherents ' and that ' no code of verbal statement can ever exhaust the shifting background of pre-supposed fact '. *Code*, originally a systematic collection of statutes and laws,

77

has come to have many applications. ' Theology offers one code ; public opinion another ; the economic system a third ; the State a fourth ' (*Belief and Action*).

All codes, however, are racially, culturally, temporally, and otherwise conditioned. To *condition*, a psychological term (especially in *conditioned reflexes* : a theory that, at the edges, is being frayed by its own inadequacy), has already gained much ground ; it often displaces ' to determine ; to mould, e.g. by the influences of environment ; to train '. (The derivative *conditioning* is almost as common.) Here are several impressive examples of its use :—' Our knowledge is conditioned by our needs as human beings ' (Inge, 1922) ; Whitehead, 1933, speaks of ' mutual behaviour conditioned by imposed laws ' and, in a metaphysical context, says that ' the laws which condition each environment merely express the general character of the occasions composing that environment ' ; ' Grantham walked slowly towards the Circus, speculating on the extent to which his decision to see Crystal had conditioned his outlook ' (Claude Houghton, 1938) ; ' At any particular time there is a conflict between the established morality and the new moral principles to which men are being gradually " conditioned " by new circumstances ' (Stapledon, 1942).

' The *ego* and the *id* ' : ' the conscious thinking subject ' and ' the instinctive impulses of the individual ' (*The Concise Oxford Dictionary*), or an individual's conscious personality and blind instincts : this remains a psychological, especially a psycho-analytical technicality ; but ' the *ego* ' has become a vogue term, ' a word of power '. Non-psychological writers sometimes extend its meaning, as in ' In many places " life " in our version [of the New Testament] represents . . ., which means the in-

dividual life—the nearest equivalent of " the Ego " '
(*Outspoken Essays*, 2nd series).

Psychology has become more complicated, more subtle,
less dogmatic. We have revolted against the excessive
bugbears and jungle-ghosts of Freud : but the residue of
Freud's teaching enables us to understand much that was
formerly obscure.

Psychosis and *neurosis* may conveniently be considered
together, as both are derangements, the former mental,
the latter functional. (Definitions of this inter-related pair
tend to differ ; and in popular usage, there is much un-
certainty as to the border-lines.) Concerning the allega-
tions of German atrocity during the war of 1914–18, *The
Daily Telegraph*, in a leader, on June 27, 1942, reminded
us that ' In this country, too, it became common form to
dismiss the stories as inventions born of a " war
psychosis " ' . *Neurosis* itself is hardly a vogue word, but
its adjective *neurotic* certainly is : witness its use in William
James's *The Varieties of Religious Experience*, in Viscount
Samuel's *Belief and Action*, and in Olaf Stapledon's *Beyond
the Isms* (' neurotic experiences studied by psychiatrists ').

Not unconnected are *repression* and *inhibition* ; (a) *complex* ; *sublimation* and *wishful thinking*. We have heard
much of the deliberate *repression* of natural impulses, and
of *inhibition*—one's instinctive or habit-induced shrinking
from a forbidden action. We have heard almost too much
of *complexes*, especially of *inferiority complex* : and far too
many of us misuse *complex* (a complete field or set of
feelings and ideas in reference to a particular subject or
emotion ; feelings and ideas not necessarily, though
frequently, abnormal) and *inferiority complex*, so often
misapprehended to denote ' an excessive sense of one's
own inferiority ', whereas it should denote the entire

field of one's feelings and ideas concerning personal inferiority—not merely the abnormality that springs from a *suppressed* sense of inferiority, even though, from the very nature of the case, we inevitably tend to concentrate upon abnormality, as in this quotation from *Beyond the Isms*. ' If, as happens to some extent to all of us, some of our frustrated sentiments '—not necessarily ignoble— ' are unconscious ; if, because they are in violent conflict with our sentiment of self esteem, we dare not recognize their existence ; if in fact they are " complexes ", they may have far-reaching and disastrous effect on our behaviour.' Two salutary examples occur in *Adventures of Ideas*. ' . . . Plato and Aristotle defined the complex of general ideas forming the imperishable origin of Western thought.'—' In every age of well-marked transition there is the pattern of habitual dumb practice and emotion which is passing, and there is the oncoming of a new complex of habit.'

Sublimation is the refined and idealized form that one can impose upon an habitual emotion or a powerful, long-enduring desire. By sublimation, love can, from selfish, become unselfish ; from predominantly physical, become predominantly spiritual. So with ambition ; so too with that restlessness which is born of excessive energy. ' The arts of civilization ', says Whitehead, ' now spring from many origins. . . . But they are all sublimations, and sublimations of sublimations, of the simple craving to enjoy freely the vividness of life which first arises in moments of necessity '.

From excessive sublimation, *wishful thinking* may arise ; not that all wishful thinking is bad ! This delightful phrase merely puts into modern phraseology the idea informing the old proverb, ' the wish is father to the thought ' : it is dangerous when it results from, or leads to, ill-founded optimism. In one place, Olaf Stapledon can write, ' Gradually scientific integrity, intellectual honesty, came to be felt as the supreme virtue, and wishful thinking became the deepest sin against the spirit ' ; in another, with equal integrity, he writes, ' My last word to the sceptic about the spirit is this. Let him earnestly examine his own heart. He has too easily cowed us by his air of superior intellectual integrity and by his imputation of confused and wishful thinking. It is time that we who recognize the spirit should have the courage of our convictions, and turn the tables on him.'

The *scientific attitude* has enabled us to learn of *space-time* and the *cosmic process* and much more about the *cosmos* itself. *Space-time* need not delay us. Sir James Jeans and Sir Arthur Eddington have entertained and excited us with spacious talk of the cosmos (the universe, not as a fortuitous concourse but as a systematic, or at least an ordered whole) and the cosmic process. ' When the average man . . . is confronted with the vastness of the cosmos as it is now revealed, he stands appalled ' (Samuel, 1937). Less appalling yet even more impressive intellectually is the process, of which Dean Inge wrote, in 1917, that ' the entire cosmic process is the life-frame of the universal Soul, the Divine Logos '. An extension of *cosmic* occurs in the following sentences :—

' It is a kind of cosmic snobbery to expect us to feel " humble " in the presence of astronomical dimensions merely because they are big ' (*Belief and Action*).

' As you get on [in years], you begin to regard the preservation of your own skin as a feat of cosmic importance ' (*Strangers*).

The *scientific attitude* has so bluffed its way into general acceptance that some people would not dream of questioning its validity. Well worth reading is Professor C. H. Waddington's *The Scientific Attitude*, a 1941 ' Pelican '. After it, however, you should, if you have not already done so, read Olaf Stapledon's chapter on the fundamental weakness of ' the sceptical scientific attitude ' (*Beyond the Isms*).

Many an *individualist* and many a believer in *self-expression, self-realization*, have rebelled against it ; above all, the individualist that possesses an adequate sense of *spiritual values* inevitably rejects its claims to sufficiency. *Individualism* is hardly a vogue word, but *individualist* and its adjective *individualistic* are so fashionable as to be powerful.

' The whole structure [of Germany in the decade preceding the war of 1914–18] was menaced by that form of individualistic materialism which calls itself social democracy ' (*Outspoken Essays*).

' From the beginning of the sixteenth century this first form of institutional civilization, with its feudalism, its guilds, its universities, its Catholic Church, was in full decay. The new middle classes, whether scholars or traders, would have none of it. They were individualists. . . . They wanted good order, and to be let alone with their individual activities ' (*Adventures of Ideas*).

Not only true individualists but also hedonists have urged the necessity of *self-realization* by *self-expression* : ' the growing emphasis of self-expression has made restraint more irksome ' (Samuel). More important is the spiritual renascence shown by the growing belief of all thinking persons in the necessity of a general re-attention to *spiritual values* and of a generally renewed fostering of *the spirit*. *Spiritual values* may be exemplified from

82

Outspoken Essays, where Dean Inge to some extent equates the spiritual with the ultimate (or absolute) values, Truth, Goodness, Beauty, and where he incidentally alludes to the former in the sentence, ' Ruskin and William Morris saw, and doubtless exaggerated, the danger to which spiritual values were exposed at the hands of the dominant economism '. *The spirit* is eloquently and vigorously defended and inculcated by Olaf Stapledon in his very remarkable little book *Beyond the Isms,* especially in Chapter III, ' The Analysis of Human Living ' ; the entire book is more profoundly Christian than 99 per cent of the works written by professed Christians. (Stapledon is an agnostic : the most spiritual of all agnostics.)

Some of the words and phrases in the group just considered might have been transferred to the third or Cultural group ; but then, several terms in the Cultural group might have been treated in the Psychological or Philosophic group, as a momentary glance at the following list will show : *escapism* (and *escapist*), *realism* (and *realist*) ; *cataclysm* ; *anti-social* ; *academic, implement* ; *significant, authentic, overtones* and *undertones* (together or separately), *prelude* ; *the Machine Age* and *Robot* (usually in the plural).

With *wishful thinking* we may compare *escapism.* This word and especially the adjective *escapist* have, since 1937, been much used in reference to literature, the theatre, the cinema, and general mentality. ' Escapism Needs Some New Twists ' is Mr. J. E. Sewell's title for his film causerie of June 29, 1942, in *The Daily Telegraph.* With *individualism* and *individualist(ic),* also of the second group, we may compare *realism* and *realist.* Since about 1930 there has been a tendency to make *realist* synonymous with ' unromantic ', ' practical ', ' hard-headed ', ' adapted—

no matter how ruthlessly—to an end ' : so much so that the mellow Viscount Samuel remarked, in 1937, that ' the peril of the modern world springs largely from the widespread belief that it is right for the individual to support action by his country which for himself would be wrong. This belief is dignified as " a sense of realism ". Name it " realism " and any wickedness becomes allowable.' And with *crisis* of the first group, compare *cataclysm*, which, in addition to being over-used, is being abused, much as *tragic* is being belittled to mean ' sad ' or even ' very unfortunate '.

Anti-social is defined by *The Concise Oxford Dictionary* as ' opposed to principles upon which society is based ' ; it has come, as in ' Professionalism always has a selfish and anti-social element in its code ' (Inge, 1917), to connote ' remote ' or ' withdrawn ' or perhaps ' specialist ', and, as in the common upper-class animadversion, ' He's an anti-social blighter ', and in *Strangers*, ' unsociable ' or ' morose '.

Somewhat similar is the recent history of *academic*, especially in such frequently employed phrases as *academic argument* (or *discussion*), *academic distinction*, *of merely academic interest*, *academic objection* (or *criticism*), and—perhaps the prototype of this phrasal set—*academic treatment* (of a subject or a problem) ; where it signifies ' remote ' or ' inhumanly cold or intellectual ' or ' logical—but impractical or impracticable ' or ' merely theoretical '. *Adventures of Ideas* (1933) affords us an excellent example, for Professor Whitehead's thinking could hardly be stigmatized as either ' wishful ' or ' sloppy '. ' The question as to the priority of the Observational Order or the Conceptual Order is, for the purpose of this discussion, academic.

An academic vogue-word of the last twenty years is (to

implement, ' to carry out (an undertaking), to achieve (a purpose) ', ' to fulfil (a promise) ' ; since about 1938, however, it has been gradually losing its magic ; it is no longer a word of power.

In the world of art and, derivatively, in the world of books, the position of *significant* roughly corresponds to that of *implement* in the academic world ; though slightly tarnished, it has retained more of its power. In 1942 Olaf Stapledon uses it effectively, basically, ' significantly ', in these two sentences :—' The whole language of religion, formerly significant, has degenerated into a mere jargon '. —' We must rediscover in our own personal lives those significant experiences which in the past gave rise to the many diverse apprehensions of the spirit.' *Authentic* attained to power only in the 1930's. In such a sentence as ' Science will not exclude the possibility of authentic messages from without ' (*Belief and Action*), or such a phrase as ' the sole authentic reality ' (*Adventures of Ideas*), there is no question of vogue : what makes of *authentic* a vogue-word is that it does duty not only for itself but also for ' real ', ' genuine ', ' indubitable ', and ' very ' (adjective) or the emphatic ' himself ', ' itself ' etc., as perhaps two brief passages from novels will suffice to indicate :—' That lovely, prim, confident word " engaged ", the word the young use about their loves, all so authentic and inevitable. Well, well.' (M. J. Farrell, *Full House*, 1935.)—' It's happening, all right. Those people . . . had the authentic stamp of actuality ' (Claude Houghton, *Strangers*, 1938).

Overtones and *undertones*, separately or in combination, are rather less fashionable than *significant* and *authentic*, but they cannot be ignored. *Undertones* was started on its vogue-career in the late 1920's with Edmund Blunden's modest masterpiece, *Undertones of War* ; overtones came a lustrum or so after *undertones*. ' Their friendship had been a light amusing lyrical affair, with no overtones or implications ' (*Strangers*, 1938). The combination has been fashionable only since about 1937.

Significant, authentic, overtones and *undertones* belong to art, literature, music ; *prelude* to literature—in music, it is a technicality. Of the many books entitled *Prelude to* . . . the most arresting is Hugh Kimber's novel, *Prelude to Calvary* ; the latest is James Reston's illuminating war-book, *Prelude to Victory*. ' To be alone . . . seemed an appropriate prelude to that final escape from the familiar which he felt was imminent ' (*Strangers*).—' I am concerned with them only as the long-drawn-out prelude to the psychological crisis of our own day, the crisis about the right kind of life for individuals and societies ' (*Beyond the Isms*).

The thinking rather than the merely cultured public raised to power—and deplored the power of—*the Machine Age* and its *Robots* ; philosophers and political thinkers authorized the phrase, and first the theatre-going (and play-reading), then the general public popularized *Robot*, from Čapek's disturbing play, *R.U.R.* or, in full, *Rossum's Universal Robots* ; both phrase and term have had a potent ' run ' of over twenty years. ' It is impossible ', wrote Dean Inge in a book published in 1922, ' not to regret the loss of handiness ' or manual skill ' which the machine age has brought with it '.—American writers have been eloquent on the theme.—And in 1938 Claude Houghton could feelingly say, ' It was so much simpler to be a brain than a man. It made one more at home in the Machine Age.'

And last the General group, falling into the sub-groups

86

of 1, Standard English words (*efficiency* ; *dynamic*, *decorative* ; *glamour* ; *intriguing* and *fantastic*, both almost slangy so recently as 1935 ; *urge* as noun ; *reaction*, generally used in the plural ; *stress*, noun ; *propaganda* ; *protagonist*) and 2, slangy or colloquial expressions (*browned off*, *that man*, *liquidate*, *operative*).

Efficiency and *efficient* are now as sledge-hammers to stun the clumsy and to daze the merely cultured, artistic, intellectual. Its correct and unobjectionable use is ex-emplified in such a statement as ' Plato then passes on to the agency whereby ideas obtain efficiency in the creative advance ' (*Adventures of Ideas*) or in such another as ' " Hope, freedom and change ", wrote Marshall, " are necessary for efficiency." They are necessary for happiness too ; but multitudes are denied them by poverty ' (*Belief and Action*). But *efficient* was gradually degraded to mean ' practical ', or ' manually or mechanically capable ', and by 1938 *efficiency* had become something of a butt to those who possessed vision, as we see from two novels published in that year : ' Her efficiency-sense is outraged ' (*Not To Be Taken*, by ' Anthony Berkeley '—the brilliant A. B. Cox) ; ' Our God is Machinery. Our trinity—Speed, Efficiency, Comfort ' (*Strangers*).

Efficiency being the cry, it is not surprising that the call is for the *dynamic* man : dynamism is the eloquence of action, the logic of hustle. Its popularity in the 1940's might have been guessed from the manner in which it was used in 1914 by Dean Inge in his Essay, *St Paul*, where he wrote, ' The Hebrew idea of God is dynamic and ethical '.

The opposite to the dynamic man is the merely *decorative* aesthete or ' lovely '. The ' lovely ' may have *glamour*, and it matters little whether she is *glamorous* in her own right or by the catch-penny arts of her dressmaker or her theatrical (or cinematographic) producer. To such power has *glamour* risen that it has not only shock-trooped its way all over the stage and film gossip and current journalism but has also invaded the vocabulary of the most reputable writers (' Love was glamour, rapture—something that made the world possible ', *Strangers*).

Intriguing is older than *fantastic* in its virtually slangy origins ; but by 1937 or so, both had so firmly established themselves in the respective senses ' fascinating or provocative or alluring ' and ' unfounded, hence imagined or imaginary ; grossly exaggerated, wildly improbable ; utterly impossible or inconceivable '. An early comment on the abuse of *intriguing* occurs in S. S. Van Dine's *The Benson Murder Case*, 1926 : ' " Rather int'restin' or, as the magazine writers say, intriguing—beastly word " '. *Intriguing*, however, is little more frequent than ' to intrigue ' : ' . . . Assisted by Mitzi willing or unwilling but no doubt intrigued ' (*Not To Be Taken*, 1938) ; ' It intrigued her imagination to visualize the slim red-haired Crystal ' (*Strangers*, 1938) ; ' Sir Thomas Browne could have propounded no more intriguing questions—intriguing just because . . .' (*The Times Literary Supplement*, June 13, 1942). *Fantastic* (literally, ' extravagantly fanciful ') may also be exemplified in a trio of quotations : ' " To us the idea that she could have poisoned John seems nothing short of fantastic " ' (*Not To Be Taken*) ; ' He was haunted by the conviction that Reality was a far more fantastic affair than most men dare to dream ' (*Strangers*). ' The Axis has suffered heavily, both in surface craft and in the air, and their major claims are roundly described by the Admiralty as fantastic ' (*The Daily Telegraph*, June 17, 1942).

Urge as a noun has gone far to displace ' eagerness ' or (strong) desire ; appetition ; (compulsive) aspiration ; (powerful) ambition : and although it is disliked by purists and by not a few others, including myself, and has, in the form *body-urge*, been satirized in that delightfully satirical novel *Cold Comfort Farm*, yet it appears in the works of numerous thinkers and writers, for example Professor Whitehead, Sir Arthur Thomson, A. B. Cox, Olaf Stapledon. ' The primary demand for freedom is to be found in the general urge for the accomplishment of the general ends, which are a fusion of ideal and economic policies, making the stuff of history '—' the creative urge ' (perhaps its best use)—' the urge towards ideal perfection ' (*Adventures of Ideas*) ; ' A physical urge, the subjective side of endeavour ' (Thomson) ; ' A first-rate man, full of the urge for adventure ' (*Not To Be Taken*) ; ' My correspondent [a Jesuit] called it an urge for the " spiritual life " or the " life of the spirit " ' and ' This disinterested urge of the actual self to destroy itself, to make way for the more awakened " self-that-might-be " ' (*Beyond the Isms*).

Reaction for ' response ', ' answer ', or even ' opinion ', and, with *on*, ' influence on ', has been extremely common since about 1930 and fairly common since about 1920. In Dr Austin Freeman's *Social Decay and Regeneration*, 1921, we read that ' Mechanism by its reaction on man, and his environment is antagonistic to human welfare ' (quoted by Dean Inge). We are almost losing sight of *reaction*, correctly used, for example, in ' Plato enunciates the doctrine that " action and reaction " belong to the essence of being ' (*Adventures of Ideas*).

Stress, as a noun, was a favourite word of Prime Minister Neville Chamberlain's, in that nuance which owes something to the influence of ' distress ' and something to that of ' strain and stress ' and ' storm and stress '. The word occurs with a rather different emphasis in ' Art can be described as a psychopathic reaction of the race to the stresses of its existence ', Whitehead, with an allusion, I think, to the phrase ' strain and stress '.

Propaganda, at its most active and dangerous in times of stress, is properly neutral (' propagation of news or opinions ') ; yet it has come to be narrowed down to the political sphere and to bear, far too often, the implication ' one-sided, exaggerated, unscrupulous, falsified '. Viscount Samuel in 1937 spoke coldly of ' Nazi or Fascist propaganda designed to influence the domestic politics of other States ' ; early in 1939 General Wavell said, ' A commander to-day now has . . . to understand something . . . of the business of propaganda ' ; and early in 1942, Olaf Stapledon sadly observed that ' Unfortunately creative imagination may be used for uncreative and lethal purposes. Such, for instance, was the use of Hitler's genius for propaganda '.

Hitler, though not originally, has long been the protagonist of Nazism, as Mussolini, his prototype, has always been the protagonist of Fascism.

Protagonist, the chief person in a drama or a story, hence the champion of a cause, is often misused to mean any notable, or indeed any, participator in a struggle, a war, a battle, a debate.

From Standard English (or its approximation) we pass to the light-hearted realm of slang and colloquialism. Our first example, however, is not so very light-hearted in its associations: the associations of *liquidation*—taken from the phraseology of bankruptcy—are grim. Viscount Samuel has referred to ' the liquidation of the kulaks '

Claude Houghton has characterized a revolutionary thus, ' Clare was Anti-Everything . . . Anyone who possessed power of any degree in any activity was listed for " liquidation " ' ; Walter Theimer uses it neutrally in his statement, ' The NEP was liquidated in 1927 and succeeded by the strictly socialistic Five-Year Plan policy '.

Another word that, becoming colloquially picturesque, has thereby gained in vogue and power is *operative*, which now so often means ' most important, most significant ', especially in the phrase, ' the operative word '; it occurs, for instance, in Nicholas Blake's *The Beast Must Die*, 1938.

' That ' is the operative word in *that man*, which has, ever since early 1940, been the most popular of all synonyms for ' Hitler ' among three-quarters of the population of Great Britain, though more among women than among men.

' That man ' is the reason why so many people are *browned off*, a phrase that is fast displacing ' fed up '. Coming from the Regular Army, it has swept through the Fighting Services and obtained a very strong hold in Civil Defence and the general citizenry. Its origin is not unconnected with ' cooked (or done) to a turn ' and ' done brown '.

July 14, 1942. Part of this essay—some two-thirds, to be precise— appeared in the January 1943 issue of *The Quarterly Review*.)

THE TEACHING OF ENGLISH
IN HIS MAJESTY'S FORCES

* * *

A REPRESENTATIVE LIBRARY

PREFACE

THIS pamphlet is based upon experience had, and on close observation made, during my four years as a private in 1915–19 and four months as a rifleman in 1940–41, and during a very much briefer period as an officer in the Army Educational Corps. But what I write here is as pertinent to the Navy and the Air Force as it is to the Army.

My main thesis : that, for our armed forces, English is not only the most important of all educational subjects but also an essential of training : may seem obvious to the thoughtful (once they have seen it set forth). But, believe me, it is anything but obvious—in practice.

The list of books I have drawn up as a basic or representative library of 100 titles does not pretend to be a list of the 100 best books ! But it will provide the serious reader with plenty to cultivate his mind and his taste ; and the confirmed fiction-reader with not only a background but also a serviceable nucleus of novels and short stories. In both the fiction and the non-fiction, I have tried to set the inexperienced reader upon the right path and to broaden the outlook of the more experienced ; also to entertain both of these kinds of reader.

April 9, 1941

The Teaching of English in His Majesty's Forces

CLEAR thinking results in clear speech or writing ; clear writing and speech pre-supposes clear thinking. But thinking can be done only with those means which are equally necessary in speech—in logically ordered words. One speaks (or writes), hence one thinks, in one's native language. For our purpose, in English. English, therefore, is the very basis—the prerequisite—of all communication, whether written (memoranda, notes, letters, indents, orders, etc.) or spoken (instructions, explanations, demonstrations, lessons). Yet, even now, you hear people say, ' Oh, but one doesn't need to *learn* English : one assimilates it.' The trouble is that everybody needs to learn at least part of his own language, however much one may assimilate ; moreover, much of the English one assimilates is bad or, at best, inferior English. Men nurtured in good homes are often astonishingly inarticulate : although they are not classified as illiterate (nor are they illiterate), they are, when they try to instruct others, as difficult to understand as those men whom we should classify as illiterate : many an officer is as hard to follow as the N.C.O. that the officer would condemn as ignorant. Indeed, an illiterate may be an effective instructor if he has the gift of vivid presentation, but it must be admitted that illiteracy usually makes for imprecision.

Clarity is essential in peace-time : in war, it is doubly necessary, for men's lives are at stake. The failure of a plan is often attributable, not to a lack of energy or in-genuity or courage in the men asked to carry out the plan, but to a faulty wording of the order or the instructions. Ambiguities produce error, variance, doubt.

Such clarity can come only from clear thinking. ' Many people cannot be taught to think clearly,' it may be said. Many ? Only the feeble-minded, the feckless, and the reckless. That ' many ' would become ' few ' if a better knowledge of words (and the simple, basic rules of every-day syntax) were taught and if, of course, the need were so emphasized that all worthy men were alive to it, hence eager to fulfil it.

Clarity is required of all ranks, and the teaching of the means to attain it should be available to the officers no less than to the men. *Every*body in His Majesty's Forces has to obey orders or put instructions into effect : it is, therefore, obvious that all orders and instruction should be written in English that is as free from ambiguity as it is possible to make it : the two great means to this end are (*a*) the correct use of words ; (*b*) the logical ordon-nance of words correctly used. Less important, but still very important indeed, is simplicity ; both in the choice of words and in syntax. Why, for instance, use the some-what affected (originally it was an academic) verb *imple-ment* for the simple *fulfil* ? Why employ sentences so long or so complex as to require careful examination and analysis before their full meaning can be grasped. (In war, it is not enough to ' have a general idea ' of what is meant : one must have a precise notion.) A Ciceronian sentence may be intellectually delightful, but in war it may waste valuable time ; it may, among the less quick-witted and intelligent, cause a misapprehension or even a grave error.

But orders are often, instructions are very often, spoken.
In speech, it is true, the long or the complex sentence is
much rarer than in writing : all the other precautions
mentioned in the preceding paragraph, however, are no
less desirable, no less necessary, in spoken than in written
orders and instructions. Oral orders and instructions have
dangers of their own. It does not help a squad when a
sergeant, taking a group of men in rifle drill, speaks of *right*
hand (or leg or side) and *left* hand (or leg or side) and
illustrates his instructions by facing the squad as he per-
forms the movement. ' But that is an example of woolly
thinking, not of woolly speaking ! ' Admittedly : but certain verbal precautions would have eased the situation.
It does not help a squad if a sergeant or an officer, very
intent on what he is doing, does not think of what he is
saying. If his mind is not at least as much on his words as
on his actions, his wording becomes imprecise and, too
often, downright hazy. It does not help a squad if a
sergeant is continually saying ' You see ' or ' Get me ? '
or if an officer continually interjects an enclitic *what* or
apologetic *don't you know* or a depreciatory *if you see what I
mean*. I have heard more than one N.C.O. blasting and
bloodying the men, more than one officer being patiently
monitory (' You're not *trying* '), when the N.C.O. or the
officer was more to blame than were the men.

The interaction, the interinfluence, of thought and
speech (or writing) can be seen in many other ways. To
give but one instance : many instructors, in detailing
some rifle or machine-gun or other weapon-training movement or even in detailing a squad movement, use technical
terms without having first explained those terms. The
particularities of movements and weapons and vehicles,
whether in the Navy, the Army, or the Air Force, are

technicalities, many of them very rarely heard outside the Services : the hard-bitten instructor, who lives with and dreams of these things, forgets this very obvious fact. Often the simplest explanation is visual : ' Have a squint down that barrel, Private Smith, and you'll see what I mean when I tell you what *rifling* is ' ; ' *This* is a magazine platform, Jorkins ' ; ' *That* is a multiple pom-pom, Jones.' The best of all explanations is the simple definition *plus* the visual demonstration. Familiarity with the meanings and implications of technical terms may degenerate into glib jargon, but even glib jargon is preferable to ignorance and confusion.

Jargon may consist in using another word for a simple, generally understood word. There is too much of this sort of thing :—' A.B. Seaman Robinson will proceed to London ' when all that is intended is that he shall *go* to London ; ' An enemy submarine was discovered [? *discerned* or merely *seen*] in a re-entrant ' (correct as a map-reading term) instead of in a *gulf*. This ' officialese ' of the Services is spreading : a pity, for it is both unnecessary and, to the plain man, far from plain. Is it necessary to teach the meaning of such jargon-words ? So long as certain officers and experts use them, it is : but need they be used ?

To return to the necessity of a better knowledge of English and to give a few instances. Every man should be able to pass a message in the exact words of the original. If a man does not know the meaning of a word, he is apt, in his effort to understand it, to forget the wording of the message itself. ' What was that you said, chum ? ' And the interrogated man, much relieved in his mind at the successful discharge of an onerous task, may in turn forget what he did say. A long word where a short one would have done equally well often causes a quite unnecessary stoppage or hitch.

Every man should be able to write a short memorandum or, less formally, a note, or to send or deliver a verbal message—perhaps a brief report or a valuable warning—of his own, for he may find himself in the position of section leader or senior soldier (or sailor or airman) ; he may be a sole survivor ; he may be asked for certain information that only he can give or, at the least, give satisfactorily. I am thinking particularly of those who are not officers, but much the same situations may confront an officer. And officers, however junior in rank, may be required to write a report or to render an oral account of an event, an incident, a position, or to propose a means of overcoming a difficulty. In all these circumstances, those officers and men who lack the ability to write or speak clearly and accurately may fairly be said to be inefficient sailors, soldiers, airmen. In that sense, therefore, the speaking and writing of clear (and preferably simple) English may be regarded as a part of naval, military, or aeronautical training. Stated thus, my contention is obvious : but there are far more persons that refuse to admit, or have not even thought of, this aspect of the subject than there are persons that admit it ; the number of those who have advocated English as a vitally necessary part of training is small.

But is there, in the course of training, time for the teaching of English ? In units actually engaged in warfare, no. In all others there should be. I do not say that English is more important than piloting to an airman, ballistics to an artilleryman or a naval gunner, the use of the rifle or the Bren gun to an infantryman, navigation to a sailor ; but I do say that it is of very great importance and that, in the *educational* programmes laid down for the members of His Majesty's Forces, it should be regarded and, what is more urgent, treated in practice as the most important of all subjects : I should, if I were asked to state my opinion unequivocally, advise that English be made an obligatory subject of instruction but that all other subjects be left, as they now are, voluntary.

At present, English is—if one is to judge by its frequency in the lists of subjects taught in classes—no more important than French or German ; and—if one is to judge by the lists of lectures—much less important than Hitler. It is like the weather in that it is taken too much for granted.

Yet good, interesting lectures could be delivered upon the subject of English ; instructive lectures ; witty lectures. For example, on ' English and French Compared ' ; ' The English and American Languages ' ; ' Official English ' ; ' Commercialese ' ; ' The Soul of Grammar ' ; ' The Fun of Word-History ' ; ' The Growth of the English Language ' ; ' Slang ' ; ' Dialect ' ; ' Dr Johnson's Life and Wit ' ; ' The History and Importance of *The Oxford English Dictionary* ' ; ' How to Read ' ; ' The Gentle Art of Letter-Writing ' ; ' The Craft of Propaganda ' ; ' How to Read a Newspaper ' ; ' Copy-Writing ' ; ' Why Write Verse ? ' ' The Trials of an Author ' ; ' A Modicum of Accidence '.

And classes in English could tackle, preferably in courses of 3–12 periods, such aspects* as these :—' Common Errors ' ; ' Illiterate Words and Phrases ' ; ' Some Very General Mispronunciations ' ; ' Elementary Syntax ' ; ' Subjunctive Mood without Tears ' ; ' How to Write a Letter *or* a Memorandum *or* a Report ' ; ' The Requisites of a War Diary ' ; ' Ambiguity and Ambigu-

* In the actual courses, simpler titles may be needed for a few of them.

ities ' ; ' Elementary Composition ' ; ' Advanced Composition ' ; ' Essay Writing ' ; ' Précis Writing '.

But what of English literature ? There is no utilitarian need for lectures or classes on and in this subject ; nor is it the concern of this pamphlet. But where there is a demand for either lectures or classes, that demand should be met. Also, certain literary subjects border on the domain of English language, English grammar, English composition. Cases in point are ' Journalism and Literature ' ; ' The Style is the Man ' ; ' How Great Writers Have Influenced the English Language ' ; ' Shakespeare ' ; ' Modern Verse '. There are many others.

The personnel for the teaching of English is available, either within the Forces or among civilians. Why not take advantage of that encouraging fact ?

APPENDIX

A few books useful to those who would teach English and to those non-beginners who wish to continue their studies privately.

The Making of English	Henry Bradley	(Macmillan)
The Growth of English	O. Jespersen	(Blackwell)
The English Language	Ernest Weekley	(In Benn's Sixpennies)
The World of Words	Eric Partridge	(Routledge)
The American Language	H. L. Mencken	(Routledge)
A Short English Grammar	O. Jespersen	(Allen & Unwin)
Advanced English Syntax	C. T. Onions	(Routledge)
The King's English	H. W. & F. G. Fowler	(Oxford University Press). Grammar and Composition

Aids to the Study and Composition of English	J. C. Nesfield	(Macmillan)
What a Word !	A. P. Herbert	(Methuen)
Modern English Usage	H. W. Fowler	(Oxford University Press). Not for beginners.
English Good and Bad	Wilfred Whitten & Frank Whitaker	(Newnes)

Dictionaries : The two best short dictionaries are *Chambers's Twentieth Century Dictionary* and *The Concise Oxford Dictionary*, both sold at 10*s.* 6*d.* ; the former published by Chambers and the latter by the Oxford University Press.

A REPRESENTATIVE LIBRARY

The publisher's name is given in parentheses : O.U.P. = Oxford University Press ; Everyman = *Everyman's Library* (J. M. Dent) ; R. = Routledge ; H.U.L. = *The Home University Library* (Thornton Butterworth).

I. NON-FICTION
(a) BASIC
1. *The Bible for To-day* (O.U.P.)
   The Bible (complete and unaltered), edited by John Stirling with excellent introductions and notes ; superbly illustrated in black-and-white.
2. *Routledge's Encyclopaedia* (R.)
3. *The Concise Oxford Dictionary* (O.U.P.)
   Be sure to get it in the latest edition.
4. *Cassell's French Dictionary* (Cassell)
   Be sure to get it in the latest edition.
5. *Cassell's German Dictionary* (Cassell)
   Be sure to get it in the latest edition.

(b) BIOGRAPHY
6. *The Concise Dictionary of National Biography* (O.U.P.)
   The British nation in its great and notable men.
7. *A Life of Jesus,* by Basil Mathews (O.U.P.)
8. *Shakespeare,* by John Masefield (H.U.L.)
9. *Napoleon,* by H. A. L. Fisher (H.U.L.)
10. *Nelson,* by Robert Southey (Everyman)

(c) HISTORY
11. *A Short History of the World* by O. Browning (Arnold)
    A stimulating work.

12. *A History of Western Civilization*
    by H. A. L. Fisher   (Arnold)
13. *A History of the Middle Ages*
    by J. W. Thompson   (R.)
    300–1500 A.D.
14. *A History of England*
    by G. M. Trevelyan   (Longmans, Green)
    Delightful reading.
15. *A History of British Civilization*
    by E. Wingfield-Stratford   (R.)
    Complementary to Trevelyan.
16. *The Martyrdom of Man*
    by Winwood Reade   (Watts)
    An arresting interpretation.
17. *The Dawn of European Civilization*
    by V. G. Childe   (R.)
18. *A History of Exploration*
    by Sir Percy Sykes   (R.)
19. *A Short History of the War of 1914–18*
    by C. R. M. F. Cruttwell   (O.U.P.)
20. *A History of France from 1870*
    by D. W. Brogan   (Hamish Hamilton)

(d) TRAVEL
21. *Modern Geography*
    by M. Newbigin   (H.U.L.)
22. *Eothen*, by A. W. Kinglake   (Everyman)
    The Middle East.
23. *Autobiography of a Super-tramp*
    by W. H. Davies   (Cape)
24. *Hills and the Sea*
    by Hilaire Belloc   (Methuen)
    A modern classic.
25. *Brazilian Adventure*
    by P. Fleming   (Cape)

(e) SCIENCE

26. *A Dictionary of Scientific Terms*
    by C. M. Beadnell (Watts)
    Small ; for the general reader.

27. *Mathematics for the Million*
    by L. Hogben (Allen & Unwin)
    Both of Hogben's books are famous—deservedly so.

28. *Science for the Citizen*
    by L. Hogben (Allen & Unwin)

29. *The Races of Europe*
    by W. Ripley (R.)
    An antidote to Aryanism.

30. *Technics and Civilization*
    by L. Mumford (R.)
    Man and the machine.

(f) LITERATURE

31. *The Works of William Shakespeare* (Blackwell)
    Very legible type ; rather heavy. Collins publish a very good, more portable edition, as also does the O.U.P.

32. *The Oxford Book of English Verse* (O.U.P.)

33. *The Oxford Book of English Prose* (O.U.P.)

34. *The Oxford Book of French Verse* (O.U.P.)

35. *The Oxford Book of Light Verse* (O.U.P.)

36. *English Prose*, 5 vols. in *The World's Classics* (O.U.P.)

37. *The Broadway Book of English Verse* (R.)
    Complementary to *The Oxford Book of English Verse*.

38. *A Dictionary of European Literature*
    by L. Magnus (R.)

39. *A Short History of English Literature*
    by A. Strong (O.U.P.)

40. *Great American Writers*
    by W. P. Trent (H.U.L.)

(g) MISCELLANEOUS

41. *The New Standard Atlas of the
    World*   (Associated Newspapers)
   The world as it was on the outbreak of war.

42. *Cassell's Classified Quotations*
    by W. Gurney Benham   (Cassell)

43. *A Dictionary of Classical Mythology* (Everyman)

44. *Songs and Slang of the British Soldier* by
    John Brophy and Eric Partridge (O.U.P.)
   1914–18 ; most of the slang is still current.

45. *The World of Words*
    by Eric Partridge   (R.)
   An introduction to language in general and to English and
American in particular.

II. FICTION

(a) THE WAR OF 1914–18

46. *All Quiet on the Western Front*
    by E. Remarque   (Putnam)
   The best-known German novel on the subject.

47. *Wooden Crosses*, by Dorgelès   (Heinemann)
   The best French novel on the subject.

48. *Rough Justice*, by C. E. Montague (Chatto & Windus)

49. *Her Privates We*
    by Frederic Manning   (Peter Davies)
   The best English novel on the subject.

50. *Vain Glory*
    ed. by G. Guy Chapman   (Cassell)
   An anthology (including non-fiction)

(b) GENERAL

   The following list is not strictly, though it is in the main,
chronological.

51. *Captain Singleton*, by Daniel Defoe (Everyman)
   As good as *Robinson Crusoe*.

52. *Gulliver's Travels*
    by Jonathan Swift   (Everyman)
53. *Joseph Andrews*, by Henry Fielding (Everyman)
54. *Humphrey Clinker*
    by Tobias Smollett   (World's Classics)
55. *Pride and Prejudice*
    by Jane Austen   (World's Classics)
    Not for sensation-seekers.
56. *Midlothian*, by Scott   (Everyman)
57. *Rookwood*
    by Harrison Ainsworth   (Everyman)
58. *Tales of Mystery and Imagination*
    by E. A. Poe   (Everyman)
    Compare No. 73.
59. *David Copperfield*
    by Charles Dickens   (Everyman)
60. *A Tale of Two Cities*, by Dickens   (Everyman)
61. *Vanity Fair*, by W. M. Thackeray   (Everyman)
62. *Tom Brown's Schooldays*
    by T. Hughes   (O.U.P.)
63. *The Scarlet Letter*
    by N. Hawthorne   (Everyman)
64. *The Woman in White*
    by Wilkie Collins   (Everyman)
65. *The Cloister and the Hearth*
    by C. Reade   (Everyman)
66. *Uncle Silas*, by J. S. Le Fanu   (World's Classics)
67. *Beauchamp's Career*   (Constable)
    The most generally readable of Meredith's novels.
68. *Under the Greenwood Tree*   (Macmillan)
    Hardy's one happy tale.
69. *Alice in Wonderland* and
    Alice through the Looking Glass
    by ' Lewis Carroll '   (Everyman)

70. *The Jungle Book*
     by Rudyard Kipling   (Macmillan)
     India.
71. *Kidnapped*, by R. L. Stevenson   (Constable)
     For most readers know *Treasure Island*.
72. *Allan Quatermain*
     by Rider Haggard   (Macmillan)
     Most readers know *King Solomon's Mines*.
73. *In the Midst of Life*
     by Ambrose Bierce   (Chatto & Windus)
     Not for the easily frightened.
74. *Sherlock Holmes*
     by Conan Doyle   (Murray)
     All the Sherlock Holmes stories.
75. *Conan Doyle's Historical Romances*   (Murray)
     Omnibus.
76. *The Forest Lovers*
     by Maurice Hewlett   (Macmillan)
77. *The Time Machine*
     by H. G. Wells   (Everyman)
78. *The Old Wives' Tale*
     by Arnold Bennett   (Everyman)
79. *Lord Jim*, by Joseph Conrad   (Everyman)
80. *Clementina*, by A. E. W. Mason   (Hodder & Stoughton)
81. *Caravan*, by John Galsworthy   (Heinemann)
     Omnibus of short stories.
82. *Trent's Last Case*
     by E. C. Bentley   (Constable)
     The best detective novel yet written.
83. *Jim Redlake*, by F. Brett Young   (Heinemann)
84. *The Father Brown Stories*
     by G. K. Chesterton   (Cassell)
     Omnibus.
85. Hugh Walpole's ' thrillers ' in 1
     volume : *Four Fantastic Tales* (Macmillan)
     Not ' deteccers '.

86. *Bulldog Drummond*, by ' Sapper ' (Hodder & Stoughton)
    Omnibus.
87. *The Four Steps*
    by John Buchan   (Hodder & Stoughton)
    Omnibus.
88. *Murder Must Advertise*
    by Dorothy Sayers   (Gollancz)
    The author's wittiest and most entertaining thriller.
89. *Meet Mr Mulliner*
    by P. G. Wodehouse   (Herbert Jenkins)
90. *Captain Hornblower*
    by C. S. Forester   (Michael Joseph)
    A stirring trilogy of the Navy in the Napoleonic Wars.
91. *Rogue Male*
    by Geoffrey Household   (Chatto & Windus)
    Far too little known.
92. *Crime and Detection*   (World's Classics)
    Two series.

Something here for everybody :
93. *Welsh Short Stories*   (Faber)
94. *Scottish Short Stories*   ,,
95. *Irish Short Stories*   ,,
96. *My Best Adventure Story*   ,,
97. *My Best Detective Story*   ,,
98. *My Best Spy Story*   ,,
99. *My Best Western Story*   ,,
100. *My Funniest Story*   ,,

(Written in April, and printed for private circulation in
May, 1941.)

From Knapsack to Baton

THE instances of a progress from private's knapsack to field marshal's baton are extremely few—except in those musical-comedy, those ' jazz ' armies in which, in South America, there are almost as many officers as men. The verbal ascent is less difficult.

A private was originally a *private soldier*, a term that seems to have come from the ranks : to do away with the implications of *common soldier* and to emphasize the fact the men were volunteers even though they were without recognized rank. To-day, however, to be a private, a gunner, a sapper, a trooper, is to have a rank. Privates insist on their little joke. If of long or meritorious service, they claim to be *full privates* or *front-rank privates*, their drill and their soldierly deportment enabling them to pass, with veteran composure, the raking glances and inquisitorial stares of the strictest inspecting officers. Recruits or slovens are apt to find themselves called *rear-rank privates* or even *lance-privates*.

The last is on the analogy of *lance-corporals*, commonly called *lance-Jacks*, those ' on appro ' corporals who do all the dirty work with little, or no, compensation. But *corporals* have authority over their sections—and better pay. *Corporal* is one of the many military terms adopted from French (Modern French *caporal*) : perhaps because he is in charge of a small *corpus* or body of men. In the vocative, to his friends, he is *corp.* Above him is the *sergeant* (in the vocative, *sarge* or *sarga* ; or, with the surname, *Sarnt*), also from French : *sergent*, from a Latin word meaning ' to serve '. As the non-commissioned officer in charge of a platoon (his commissioned overman being the lieutenant), he is a man of some weight. The *sergeant-major* (literally, ' greater sergeant ') was originally of commissioned rank ; whether C.S.M. or R.S.M., he is, as it were, a non-commissioned adjutant, whereas the old *colour-sergeant* carried the regimental colours or standard.

Coming to officers—in ascending order : subalterns ; captains ; field officers ; general officers—we pass from lieutenants and captains to their superiors. A *lieutenant* (slangily a *loot*) is the French for ' place-holder ', with which compare the synonymous Latin *locum tenens* : he is the representative of a higher authority : a field officer's deputy. Beginning as a second lieutenant with one star, he becomes a first lieutenant with two stars : from a *one-pipper* (not, as in the last war, ' one star, one stunt ') he becomes a *two-pipper*. First and second lieutenants are generically *subalterns* or ' inferiors '—and addressed as *Mr.*

A *captain*, who may, or may not, have charge of a company (a *company commander*) or is perhaps an adjutant, derives his title from the French *capitaine* (Italian *capitano*) ; he is a chief, the word coming from Latin *caput*, the head ; ' the heads ', in slang, are one's remote superiors. An *adjutant* is that officer who is the maid of all work : he *helps* the battalion commander : Latin *adjutans*, ' (a man) helping '. In the 18th century, he was also called an *aide-major* ; and as Captain Francis Grose, who in addition to writing on slang and antiquities, including military history, held two adjutancies in the 1760's and 1770's, has remarked, ' There is scarce any duty going forwards in a regiment, without the adjutant having some share in it '.

Major, literally ' greater (officer) ', is the lowest rank of field officer. His, too, is a title adopted from French and coming ultimately from Latin, *major* being the comparative of *magnus* (great). Carrying a crown on the shoulder of his uniform, he is a man of importance : and by virtue of his rank, he used to pass straight into *Who's Who*. Above him is a *lieutenant-colonel*, ' one who takes the place of a colonel '. He may or may not be in charge of a battalion, whereas a *colonel* has charge of a battalion or even, until his promotion goes through, of a brigade. Before about 1650, he was *coronel*, a French word derived —via Spanish—from Italian *colonnello* (in charge of a *colonna*, a column or a regiment) ; the form in -*r* was partly caused by folk-etymology association with Latin *corona*, a crown. He commands the basic infantry unit : a regiment or a battalion. And by the way, the term *regiment* has changed considerably in meaning ; now old-fashioned, when not traditionally titular, for a battalion, it once was used also for what we nowadays call a brigade (of infantry). Etymologically, it is a unit *ruled* (Latin *regimen*), whereas *battalion* is a *battling*, fighting, unit. A *regiment of foot*, or *of the line*, was an infantry as opposed to a cavalry regiment (*of horse*).

Now for General Officers : all the ranks above a *colonel*. A *General* commands an *Army* (' General Gough of the Fifth Army '), the largest component of the *Forces* (*force*, power or strength), and the word occurred, at first, only in combination—*captain general, colonel general, ser-geant-major general ;* as still in *brigadier general, lieutenant general, major general ;* compare *chaplain general* and *quarter-master general*, supreme chaplain and supreme quarter-master. Oddly enough, a lieutenant general is of higher rank than a major general, for whereas the former com-

mands an Army Corps, the latter commands a Division
a Brigade has a brigadier general. *General* comes, vi
French, from Latin *generalis*, ' concerning the *whole* of
class or kind '.

The general formerly designated the commander of the
entire military forces of a state. But the *commander in chie*
(he who, at the head of the army, puts his hands to the
work : *manus dat*) has now the rank of *field-marshal*, a
designation bestowed also on several General Officers of
royal degree or particularly distinguished service, as an
honorary title ; ' the field marshal ', however, is the
commander in chief : the Italian *Generalissimo*. At first
he was, in the English army, that staff officer who had
charge of the army's sustenance and camping-arrange-
ments. *Field* refers to the field of battle ; *marshal* is of
lowly origin, the word originally meaning, in Old English,
a horse-servant ; as a military title, *field marshal* comes
from the modern German *Feldmarschall*, and was not
used in England until two centuries ago, or some ninety
years after the Civil War, the war during which, or as a
result of which, so many military titles took on a sense the
same as, or at the least approximating to, the modern one,
as perhaps did *quartermaster* (originally a naval term with
a slightly different origin)—the officer that, known as
' the quarter bloke ', is in a battalion the *master* of *quarters*,
as in *Army Headquarters*.

The Napoleonic Wars and the military reforms of the
early 1880's finally determined the exact sense of all the
words noted here, whether of *rankers* (privates and non-
commissioned officers ; hence, officers risen from the
ranks) or others.

(Written in 1939.)

War as a Word-maker

WAR, decimator of nations and desolation of women, has ever been an augmentor of vocabulary. We see it in Greek and Latin and in every modern language. The Dutch Wars and the Napoleonic, like the Crimean and the Mutiny of the 1850's, brought their accretions. Let us, however, pass to the 1880's.

War introduces names of new weapons, instruments, implements, tactics, formations ; it also introduces or popularizes the names of new peoples, geographical or topographical features, customs and other social and sociological features, and it is mainly these latter which have entered the language from foreign sources.

The Sudan campaigns, which so long went against us, introduced or popularized *Fuzzy-Wuzzy*, *mullah*, *wadi*, *zariba*.

Fuzzy-Wuzzy, originating as British soldiers' slang, soon became a journalistic, hence a general colloquialism for the combatant Sudanese dervish, who, as those who saw the film entitled *The Four Feathers*, will remember, had an—as Kipling phrased it—' 'ayrick 'ead of 'air'. Compare *fuzzy*, ' fluffy ', and *fuzz-ball*, ' puff-ball ' ; *fuzz* is an echoic word, ' imitative of blowing away light particles ' (Weekley).

The British public, hearing of the Mad Mullah, wanted to know what *mullah* could mean anyway, and duly learned that it was a Mohammedan honorific accorded to certain ecclesiastical dignitaries ; the more educated even absorbed the fact that, in Arabic (whence the term derived), *maula* represents a magistrate, a judge, also a master, a lord.

Of *wadi* we have heard much in the present war, but it had become quite widely known in the distant 1880's. From the Arabic, it means ' water-course or river-bed ', and it is properly applied to those streams which exist in the rainy season and, in the dry, simply are not—rather, therefore, to the course or bed than to the water. *Zariba* in its more exact phonetic form, *zareeba*, signifies a fenced camp ; the ' fence ' may—and usually did—consist of bushes, especially thorn-bushes, or other haphazard material (remember *The Four Feathers* ?). Again the origin is Arabic : *zariba*, ' pen ' or ' fold ' for livestock.

The Zulu wars definitely popularized *assagai* and *impi*, earlier known only to South Africans, hunters, and insatiable readers of travel-books, and it was through them rather than by the Boer War that we acquired *sjambok*, that South-African Dutch word which, probably brought by Portuguese traders, had migrated from India, the effective origin being the Urdu *chabuk* ; the manly Zulu resented the use upon their bodies of this heavy whip made of hide. *Assagai* (frequently *assegai*), that throwing spear of South African tribes which was especially danger-ous when propelled by the thewy arms of a hefty Zulu (see, for instance, Rider Haggard's *King Solomon's Mines*), likewise travelled with the Portuguese from Asia to Africa ; Purchas, in his *Pilgrimage*, had used it, not far short of three hundred years earlier, in reference to Guinea, and in a different form (*launcegay*) it had occurred in Chaucer's *The Canterbury Tales*. Ultimately, *assagai* transliterates the Arabic *az zaghayah*, *az* for *al* (' the ') preceding the Berber name for the weapon itself ; the European shapes, *launce-*

gay (or *lancegay*) and *archegaye* (with several variants), have obviously dropped the merely prelusive ' the '-part of the combination, and these shapes originated with the Moors in Spain, the Moors having adopted the weapon from the Berbers. ('Dear me,' said the dear old lady, ' what a lot of history comes into it ! ') The history of *impi* is much briefer, its etymology much simpler : meaning, to us, ' Zulu army ', *impi* is merely the Zulu word for ' company of people ; especially if they are armed '. Of these three words, by the way, Skeat records only one, whereas Weekley includes precisely three.

Nor does Skeat deign to notice *commando*, so often heard, against us, during the Boer War and, in a rather different sense, used by us, during the latter half of the Second World War : the first word in the list of Boer War acquisitions. There is, thus entitled, a famous book by a Boer that, having fought most gallantly against us, now supports us most loyally.

Like *sjambok, assagai, kraal* and (untreated here) *dervish, commando* migrated from Asia to Africa on the ships of the shrewd and venturesome Portuguese traders, but *commando* (' body of troops called out for service and under one command ') differs from the other terms in this, that whereas they were originally Asiatic, it is originally Portuguese (from, as usual, the Latin) ; for comparative purposes, one may adduce *Commander of the Faithful*, the English translation of the title assumed, somewhere about the year 640 A.D., by Caliph Omar I. The British Commandos or initial-assault troops, like their American counterparts the Rangers, vie in daring and hardiness with their Boer prototypes ; the British have learnt many useful military lessons from their former foes.

Other words current at the time of the Boer War

(1899–1902), some of them now obsolescent in Britain and a few of them mentioned only in this incomplete alphabetical list, are *dissel-boom, klipspringer, kloof, kopje, kraal, kranz* or *krantz, laager, predikant, span* of oxen with its derivatives *inspan* and *outspan, trek* and its derivative *voortrekker* (with which compare *voorlooper*), *trippel, veldt* (whence *veldt-kornet* and *veldtschoen*), *vlei* ; and the two slang terms, *mafficking* and *stellenbosch*.

A *klipspringer* is a South African antelope, an animal that some of those wily, wiry Boer commando-troops uncomfortably resembled. A Dutch word, it literally means 'cliff-springer'. *Disselboom* belongs to the trekking group of Boer words, for it is what we should call the waggon-pole ; it is Dutch for 'shaft-*beam*'. *Trek* itself derives from Dutch *trekken*, 'to drag, to draw (a vehicle)' ; hence, 'to journey by ox-drawn waggon' ; *trekken* comes from the Latin *trahere*, 'to draw (a load)'. From *trek* comes *voortrekker*, from Dutch *voortrekken*, to journey in advance : a *voortrekker* is a pioneer, an early Dutch settler in South Africa ; comparable is *voorlooper* ('a forerunner'), already obsolescent in Britain. Those pioneers and their descendants inspanned and outspanned their oxen. Owing to Dutch influence, *span* was early used of harnessing horses and putting them to a cart or a waggon, a sense reintroduced, as Weekley has observed, from South Africa. The root-idea of the noun *span* is : stretching from one point to another, as it also is in the verb ; compare the Biblical *span of life*, stretching from birth to death ; the Vulgate version is *dies mensurabiles* (literally, measurable days). On those long, thirst-perilous treks across the veldt, the oxen had to be most carefully inspanned and most solicitously outspanned (unharnessed and tethered), for the South African *veldt*, defined by

Skeat as ' an open grassy tract of country ', annotated by Weekley in the terms ' for South African sense, cf. *prairie* ', and defined by *The Little Oxford Dictionary* as ' tract of land with little or no forest ; wild grassland ', can become almost as dry as a desert and, for brief periods, almost as waterless. *Veldt* is the older form of Dutch *veld*, ' field ', the Dutch being, radically, the same word as Old English *feld* (modern ' field '). Whence *veldtschoen*, literally ' field-shoes ', those strong, handsome, durable shoes which England now manufactures in imitation of the even stronger, the less elegant Boer original.

Geographical features have given us *kloof, kopje, kranz, vlei*, of which only the second has, in Britain, remained current. *Kloof*, a ravine, is Dutch for a cleft and therefore related to *cleave*, ' to split '. *Kopje*, Dutch for ' a small hill ', is a diminutive of *kop*, ' head ' (as in Spion Kop, which so many Englishmen ceased, precisely there, to remember) ; compare Old English *cop*, ' top (especially of a hill) '. The Dutch and English words derive from Latin *cupa*, ' a bowl ', with particular reference to the top of an inverted bowl or cup. *Kranz* or *krantz*, an overhanging rock-face, represents the true Dutch *krans*, ' a coronet '. A *vlei, vley, vly*, a ' depression ; hence, a swamp ', represents a contraction of Dutch *vallei*, ' a valley ', with which compare French *vallée*.

From geographical to social features. *Kraal*, a fenced South African native village, also an enclosure for cattle, occurs in some Voyages published in mid 18th century, thus, ' This shews the *koral*, or *kraal*, to be a village '. The etymological chain appears to be : Dutch *kraal*, from Portuguese *curral* (cattle enclosure, sheepfold) with an influencing by Spanish *corral*, from Latin *currere*, ' to run ' (compare *sheep-run*). The predominant sense would seem to originate immediately in the Spanish phrase *correr toros*, literally ' to run bulls ' but idiomatically ' to hold a bull-fight '. A *laager* is a circular encampment, especially a temporary encampment, whose circumference consists of ' outspanned ' waggons ; hence, *laager*, ' to form or place in a laager '. South-African Dutch *lager*, from Dutch *leger*, ' a camp '. Cognates are *leaguer* (implied in ' a beleaguered garrison ') and *lair*.

Thus we arrive at one unclassifiable and two slang words. A *predikant* is a Protestant minister and the word is Dutch, from *predigen*, ' to preach ' (Latin *prae* + *dicare*, to proclaim). *Mafficking*, applied to the delirious rejoicing at the relief, on May 17, 1900, of Mafeking, so skilfully defended by Baden-Powell, has generated, by back-formation, the verb *maffick*, ' to rejoice riotously ', now obsolescent. *Stellenbosch* is Army slang for ' to relegate to a place where incompetence is less harmful. From *Stellenbosch*, Cape Colony, said to have been used for this purpose in Kaffir Wars' (Weekley) ; the term was revived during the Boer War. As Professor Weekley remarks, the explanation perhaps lies rather in the fact that even in the late 18th century, Stellenbosch was regarded as an asylum for old age—a reputation for which it no longer qualifies.

The Russo-Japanese War introduced or popularized such words as *banzai*, *bushido*, *hara-kiri*, *Samurai* : but, being a foreign not a domestic war, that national quarrel left a much slighter impression on the English language than did wars in which Britain herself was engaged.

The war of 1914–18 considerably influenced English ; so considerably that, here, this influence must be treated with comparative brevity. To English slang, it added several hundred words. Except to a very minor degree, however, we are not concerned with slang.

From German came such words and phrases as *according to plan, achtung, ersatz, frightfulness, hate, kamerad !, kultur, strafe, sunk without trace, contemptible little army.*

According to plan is a translation of the German *plangemäss*, which, in 1918, was, by apologists, much used of yielding ground. In English mouths it assumed an ironic tinge and among officers it was employed jocosely. *Achtung !* simply means ' Attention ! ' or ' Be careful ! ', as in *Achtung minen*, ' Look out for mines '. *Ersatz* is annotated thus by Professor Weekley, ' *ersatz* [neologism]. Ger., replacement, from . . . *setzen*, to set, place.— " There will be [in Germany] much ersatz democracy to admire " (*Daily Chronicle*, Sept. 23, 1918).' By most Englishmen, including prisoners of war in Germany in 1916–18, it was apprehended as ' substitute ', hence also as ' temporary, provisional ', as in ' *ersatz girl* ', a German girl as pass-time. Of the phrase *contemptible little army*, Weekley (1921) has, in reference to the adjective, pungently written and most appositely quoted as follows : ' Used (since Sept. 1914) to render German *verächtlich*, an epithet oddly applied by Wilhelm II of Germany to the finest army that ever took the field. Cf. *frightfulness*.— " This makes me naturally love a souldier, and honour those tattered and contemptible regiments that will dye at the command of a sergeant " (*Religio Medici*) ' : with which compare the Duke of Wellington's phrase, uttered a few days before Waterloo, ' infamous army ' (see Georgette Heyer's arresting novel, *The Infamous Army*), and A. E. Housman's verses to an army of mercenaries. *Frightfulness* renders the German *Schrecklichkeit*, which, on August 27, 1914, was officially applied ' to the intimidation of a neutral civilian population by outrage, massacre and the destruction of historic buildings and artistic treasures'; thus Weekley, who, from Brand-Whitlock's *Belgium under German Occupation*, quotes thus, ' Louvain will remain, perhaps, the classic instance of *Schrecklichkeit* . . . But it was not the worst '. The slang use of *hate* for a bombardment, as in ' the usual morning hate ', contains an allusion to Lissauer's *Hymn of Hate* (August 1914) ; related is *strafe*, ' to subject (the enemy) to a bombardment ', and its derivative noun, ' From German phrase *Gott strafe England*, " God punish England ", a common salutation in Germany in 1914 and the following years' (*The Oxford English Dictionary*). Such words reveal the nature of German *Kultur*, ' identical in origin, but not in sense, with *culture* ', as Weekley pithily remarks before he quotes Freytag-Loringhoven's ' The vast distance between civilisation and kultur was closely revealed ', as the next generation also came to realize. *Sunk without trace*, a neat example of *kultur*, renders the official German phrase for a ship sunk by a German submarine. But even a German has at last to cry *Kamerad !*, ' Comrade, spare me ', when retribution overtakes him.

Of the rather more numerous adoptions, adaptations and ' Hobson-Jobson's ' of French words, we will take only a few : *camouflage* and *espionage*, *dégommé* and *embusqué*, *napoo* and *finee*, *estaminet* and *promenade*, and *san fairy ann*. The first pair represents popularization ; the second pair, upper-class slang : the third, soldiers' slang, as also is *san fairy ann* ; the fourth, adoptions.

Of *camouflage*, originally from the slang of the lively, vivid, ingenious Parisians, with its *camoufler*, ' to disguise ', perhaps from Italian *camuffare*, ' to disguise ' (not improbably for *capo muffare*, ' to muffle the head '), Ernest Weekley has noted that it ' was naturalized with amazing rapidity early in 1917 ' and quotes Mr G. B. Shaw as saying ' I was in khaki by way of camouflage' (*The Daily Chronicle*, March 5, 1917). *Espionage*, known long before, was popularized by the war; it is the French *espionnage*, from *espion*, 'a spy' (Italian *spione*); the operative Romance origin is Latin *specere*, 'to look'.

Dégommé, 'relieved of one's command', 'relegated to a comparatively unimportant position,' sometimes with the implication 'dismissed the service', has, for its former and predominant sense, an exact parallel in the English slang *come unstuck* and, for its latter, in the equally slangy *bowler-hatted*; after all, the literal meaning of *dégommé* is 'ungummed'. Earlier equivalents are, in English, *Stellenbosched* (which we have already met) and, in French, *Limogé* ('sent to Limoges'). *Dégommé* is, in the main, an officers' and middle-class word, as also is *embusqué*, of which Weekley has written that, 'In sense of one avoiding the front, this is a neologism from French *s'embusquer*, "to lie in wait",' and it was applied not only to the Serviceman in a 'cushy' job but to the Civil Serviceman sheltering from the army, what we in England used to call a *Cuthbert*.

Napoo and *finee* are slang synonyms in the sense, 'finished, ended', but *napoo* also means 'hopelessly wounded or disabled; dead' and 'sold out; no longer available'. The British soldier had so often heard *Il n'y en a plus* (there's no more of it; there's none left) from the mouths of French shop-keepers that he adopted it; Weekley has aptly said that *napoo* was 'regarded by Mr Atkins as a current French phrase closing a discussion in indefinite fashion' and quotes *The Pall Mall Gazette* of February 15, 1917, thus, 'Not the napoo victory ensuing from neutral pressure and semi-starvation, but the full decisive military victory'. *Finee*, obviously, is the French *fini*.

If he went for a *promenade* or a walk, Tommy Atkins usually hoped to end-up at an estaminet, the nearest approach to his beloved ' pub ' ; an *estaminet* is properly a humble café with a smoking-room, and its origin is still obscure. Apropos of *promenade*, used also as a verb equivalent to the French *faire une promenade*, his usual address to a pretty or otherwise attractive girl or woman with whom he hoped to ' click ' took the form, *Mam'selle* (or *Mademoiselle*), *promenade ?*

But whatever he was doing, whatever the difficulty or the hardship or the danger, the British soldier tended to shrug his shoulders in a manner comically imitative of that of the expressive Frenchman and say, *san fairy ann* (or *Anna*) *!*, which re-shapes the French *ça* (for *cela*) *ne fait rien*, ' it makes no matter—it makes no difference—it doesn't matter—what's the odds ? ' Hugh Kimber, the author of that brilliant and very moving story, *Prelude to Calvary*, not long after the war of 1914–18 published a novel entitled *San Fairy Ann*.

From Hindustani and Egyptian Arabic several terms came into common English idiom : *Blighty* and *cushy* ; *bint* and *maaleesh* : all of them slang, but the first pair very widely used indeed. *Blighty*, ' England ' (or ' Britain ') and ' English ', arrived via the Regular Army men, who took it from the Urdu *bilati*, Arabic *wilayati*, ' governmental ' ; *wilayat* means ' government ', hence ' the British government ', hence ' England ' or ' Britain '. In *Hobson-Jobson*, published late in the 19th century, we read that ' The adjective *bilayati* or *wilayati* is applied specifically to a variety of exotic articles '. The British soldier also spoke of ' a Blighty wound ' or one that would cause him to be sent to a hospital in Britain : the German soldier, as Professor Weekley reminds us, used the equivalent *Heimatschuss*, literally ' a home-shot '. In hospital, one had ' a cushy time ' ; a man at a base-camp had ' a cushy job ', and in *The Daily Express* of February 7, 1917, a journalist pointedly said that ' The making of cushy jobs in these days of labour famine is an evident evil '. By folk-etymology, *cushy* has been associated, perhaps as a telescoping of *cushiony*, with cushions, but more probably it originated in a Hindustani word deriving from the Persian *khush*, ' pleasure '. Less general than *Blighty* and *cushy* are the two words direct from the Arabic spoken in Egypt : *bint*, ' a girl ' (as opposed to *walad*, ' a boy ', with which compare the Hindustani *wallah*), *Saïda, bint* (' Good-day, lass ! ') being a common form of greeting ; and *maaleesh*, the neat equivalent of *san fairy ann*, although connoting a more easy-going attitude of mind, for the full Arabic equivalent of *san fairy ann* is *Kismet* !

Nor should we forget that as the present war has grafted on the English stock a useful pair of words, *jeep* and *G.I.* (strictly, ' general issue ' as applied to clothing, etc., etc., etc., but loosely ' an ordinary American soldier '), so that of 1914–18 familiarized us with *Doughboy*, for an American soldier. *Doughboy* seems to have begun its military career during the American Civil War, ' a nickname from the shape of the buttons originally worn by the regular army suggesting the kind of biscuit called a *doughboy* in U.S. and 17th-century England ' (Weekley).

And from the Spanish Civil War of the 1930's we have received the doubtful advantage of *fifth column*, with its derivative *fifth-columnist*, of an ' organized body sympathizing with and working for the enemy within countries at war ; loosely, traitors, spies' (Addenda, 1941, to *The Little Oxford Dictionary*).

But what of the war of 1939? We are perhaps too close

to assess the linguistic gains to be snatched from the Martian maelstrom in respect of such words and phrases as *encirclement* and *peaceful penetration* and *Lebensraum*; *Weltpolitik* and *Herrenvolk* and *Führer*, *Gestapo* and *purge*, *Aryan* and *strength through joy*, *Wehrmacht* and *Luftwaffe* and '*to Rotterdam*' or '*Coventrate*', *Panzer* and *Blitzkrieg* and its derivative *blitz*, both noun and verb; *Maginot Line* and *do a Dunkirk* and *Maquis*. That, as the teasing anecdotists say, is another story.

(Written in October 1944.)

Thanks to the War . . .

(1939–1945)

WITH A NOTE ON REFERENCE BOOKS FOR NEOLOGISMS

WAR is a powerful excitant, perhaps the most rapidly effectual excitant, of language. It quickens and enlivens, enriches and invigorates language as much in the 20th century as exploration and travel used to do in the 16th–17th centuries. That is not a justification, it is an inevitable result, of war—at least of any modern war that has lasted more than a few months.

In the war of 1939–45, as in that of 1914–18, the fighting Services have experienced a far more extensive enrichment of their vocabularies, whether technical or unconventional, than the civilian or social services have experienced ; many Service terms, however, soon find their way into the civilian vocabulary. ' In the Services, the men [and the women] live—or should live—a more exciting life ; they deal with new equipment and various weapons ; do things they've never done before . . . ; many of them visit strange countries ; many become engaged in a service that is actually instead of nominally active ; all of them mingle in such a companionship as they have never had before they enlisted and will never again have, once they quit the Service.

' Such conditions inevitably lead to a rejuvenation of language—to vividness—to picturesqueness—to vigour ; language becomes youthful, energetic, adventurous.' (From the introduction to *A Dictionary of R.A.F. Slang*.)

But civilians have, in the recent ' spot of bother ', been involved as never before : to pass through a *blitz* is unpleasant ; yet, as an old lady of the East End remarked in December 1940, ' it does take your mind off your worries '.

The words that are to be briefly treated here have been selected to fit a chronological arrangement. Some of them refuse to fit. Nevertheless, they do belong where I've put them, whenever or wherever else they may assert themselves—as words have a way of asserting themselves. But it is only a selection.

The Spanish Civil War, lasting from July 18, 1936, to April 4, 1939, constituted, although only the Axis powers seem to have been aware of the fact, that rehearsal, that Martian pre-view, of the impending World War which has been admirably related in J. Alvarez del Vayo's *Freedom's Battle*. The original *Fifth Column* consisted in the Franco sympathizers within Madrid and it was General Mola who, leading four columns of troops against the city, thus described them in a wireless address ; hence, *fifth column*, ' secret subverters and sympathizers ', any one of them being a *fifth-columnist*. In that stylistic exemplar of compression, *The Civilization of Spain*, Professor J. B. Trend spoke of Philip of Spain's sympathizers in pre-Armada England as ' a " fifth column " '.

Far closer attention was paid, in Great Britain, to the Hitler-generated ' alarums and excursions ' : the days of *Weltpolitik* and *Machtpolitik* (the latter more usual in its translation, *power politics*), of *encirclement* and *protective custody*, of *appeasement* and *peace in our time*, and of *Rassentheorie* with its perversions of *Aryan* and *Semitic*. But into that Jungian maelstrom of Teutonic delusion and British procrastination I prefer, uncontroversially, to refrain from

128

ılunging ; the hysteria of the *Herrenvolk* does not appeal
o me, nor yet the other thing. If you, however, wish to
ılunge, then take, as companions, Walter Theimer (here-
nafter mentioned) and the R. G. Collingwood of *The New
Leviathan*.

On September 1 (merely confirmed by September 3),
1939, many of us said, ' This is it ! ' and on September 4,
we bought *black-outs* for the windows ; we became experts
n the art of *blacking-out*. Rather earlier was the aviators'
black(-)out, noun and verb, ' (to experience) a temporary
loss of consciousness, especially during a long power-
dive ', but it was only in 1940 that this technical sense
became public property. For some eight months, the self-
deluders spoke of ' the *phoney* war ' (*phoney* being American
slang from the American underworld, earlier the English
underworld) and restored that expressive word to the
British vocabulary. But, Hitler ready, the storm broke—
where no storm had been feared by the credulous. Nations
fell. Thanks, in the main, to the *quislings*. Rarely has a
word so quickly and so firmly grasped the world's
imagination as this common-propertying of the Proper
Name, ' Vidkun *Quisling* '. This Norwegian ex-Army
officer, turning politician, turning traitor, was executed in
1945 at the age of fifty-eight, but not before he had, in
April, 1940, done his country a great wrong. *The Little
Oxford Dictionary*, 3rd edition, 1941, classified it as slang,
but by—indeed, well before—the end of the year it had
been admitted to Standard English.

Within a month of Quisling's manifested treachery, we
had another neologism—' to *Rotterdam* ', to which the
bombing of Britain added ' to *Coventrate* (better, *coventrate*)'.
Whereas the former term means ' to obliterate—or
attempt to obliterate—a vital portion—a clearly indi-

cated area—of a city', the latter means ' to (attempt to) destroy an entire city ', as citizens of Coventry are un-likely to forget.

A notable element in German efficiency was that of the *Panzerdivision* or, as we know it, *Panzer division*, ' armoured division '. The word *Panzer* has nothing to do with *panthers*, that idea being folk-etymology that arose from an association of not grossly dissimilar sounds and the swiftness of panthers and Panzers. Literally, *Panzer* is ' armour '; in combination it is equivalent to ' armoured '. The German word was used so much, not only in May–June 1940 but again in North Africa, that it was adopted by the troops, as in ' Here come the Panzers ! ' British pluck not long availed against the Germans in the spring of 1940, and at the end of May the B.E.F. had to *do a Dunkirk* in grim fact (see, above all, A. D. Divine's *Dunkirk*) ; the phrase was painfully repeated in connexion with the departures from Greece and Crete (see especially James Aldridge's *Signed with Their Honour* and *The Sea Eagle*), much less painfully when the Axis troops were prevented from 'doing a Dunkirk' : effecting a sea-borne withdrawal against heavy odds. So ended the *Blitzkrieg* or ' lightning-war '.

But not *Blitzkrieg* itself, for, in a shortened form and a different sense, it dominated the next period, the Battle of Britain and the bombing of Britain, especially *the London blitz* : August 1940–May 1941, with isolated *Baedeker raids* on places of tourist interest, especially cathedral cities, later. In *The* (New York) *Nation* of November 9, 1940, Lester V. Berrey, American scholar, in an article, ' English War Slang ', wrote : ' The word that has received the greatest currency at home and abroad is *blitz*, used as both noun and verb. It carries the impli-

ation of bombardment on a much grander scale than the
1914[-1918] contribution of *strafe*, and will probably find
as permanent a place in the language of war.' Like *strafe*,
it has also been used derivatively, both as noun and as
verb, for ' (to deliver) a severe reprimand (to a person) '.
For millions of people, the *blitz* has invested such simple
words as *siren, alert, all-clear*, with an emotional content, a
tremendous significance these words had not previously
possessed, and, as to millions the Blitzkrieg had trans-
formed *refugee* from a colourless to a dolorous word, so to
millions the *blitz* has familiarized *evacuee*, which, however
horrible a derivation from ' evacuated person ' (itself a
poor substitute for ' transferred person ' or some richer
term), has been forced upon us by usage. It was also
during this period, latter 1940–early 1941, that *fighter*
became established for ' fighter 'plane ' and *bomber* for
' bomber (or bombing) 'plane ', to such an extent that
these are now almost the predominant senses of those two
words.

To the earlier part of this period we owe the expressive
take evasive action. Mary Welsh Monks, in her article, ' No
Time for Tears ', in Allan A. Michie & Walter Graebner's
Lights of Freedom, 1941, conveniently stated that ' Fighter
pilots' combat reports include " I took evasive action ",
and the W.A.A.F. adopted it in describing their adventures on dates. It is heard in powder rooms everywhere
now '—*powder room* being an import from the United
States. In 1941–42 it signified (as it still does), ' to avoid
a difficulty or a danger ; to depart tactfully, or prudently
escape '. Since early 1943 it has also signified, ' to evade
payment of a debt or the discharge of an onerous or
unpleasant duty '.

Let us, before we pass to another Service and to other

periods, discharge our neological debt to the Royal Air
Force and its fellows, chiefly the R.A.A.F., the R.C.A.F.
the R.N.Z.A.F., the R.S.A.A.F., and note a few of the
inceptions made by, or because of, the Air Force. One of
the most enduring is *flak*, which began as slang and as a
toast (' Here's flak '—instead of *mud*—' in your eye ! '), so
very quickly became jargon, or official technicality, and
by late 1943 formed a reputable ingredient of the language
for ' anti-aircraft fire or guns '. Its four letters represent
the initials of the elements in the German compound noun
' *Fl*ieger*a*bwehr*k*anone '. It took more than flak to send
our bomber pilots into *a flat spin* (or fluster), which is a
revival from the R.F.C.—R.A.F. slang of 1914–18. Of one
who failed to return from a sortie, his companions remarked that he had *gone for a Burton*, the reference being
to ale. *He's* (or *You've*) *had it* !, on the other hand, means
not that ' He's copped it ' but that he will have to go
without something : in other words, ' He hasn't had it—
and won't get it ' ! An ironic expression.

Such irony may be postulated to move gremlins to work
the mischief that airmen have, for some years, been
asserting is constantly being done by these sprites. The
gremlins are reputed to be a foot high, to be diabolically
mischievous, and to sit or stand about grinning and
grimacing at the aircrew they have so gravely incon-
venienced by interfering with the mechanism of the 'plane
while it was flying. The gremlin belongs to what we
might rather fatuously call ' a conscious, or deliberate,
piece of folk-lore '. The origin of the term is obscure.
Webster's New International Dictionary says, ' Perhaps from
Irish *gruaimin*, ill-humoured little fellow, by confusion
with *goblin* '. That is an ingenious theory, and perhaps
correct ; certainly there is either confusion, or a blending,

with *goblin*, for the gremlin is a Puck-like imp. My own theory is that *gremlin* is a blend of *grim*acing (or *grin*ning) gob*lin*. Against the wiles of gremlins, even a Mae West is sometimes useless.

Already current in 1939 was *Mae West*, the life-jacket worn by aircrews. Beginning as slang, in reference to that famous film actress's vital buxomness, it had, by late 1942, become the official term. Earlier—probably since about 1930—is *gen*, ' information, or instructions ', and it derives not, as so often stated, from ' genuine ', but from that sacrosanct phrase, ' for the *general information* of all ranks '. But *gen* has always been slang. To the deepest jargon, however, belongs *cannibalization*, ' the use of parts from various damaged or other unserviceable, or at the least no longer or not yet operational, aircraft ' : one 'plane eating many others.

Aircraft? 'plane? Early in 1943 the Air Ministry decreed that an *aeroplane* was now to be an *aircraft* (plural, *aircraft*) and an *aerodrome* an *airfield*. The names of aircraft hardly concern us here, but it is worth noting that whereas the Germans name their aircraft after the designers or occasionally the manufacturers, as in *Junkers* (not *Junker*), *Dornier*, *Heinkel*, *Henschel*, *Messerschmitt*, *Focke-Wulf*, we ignore our brilliant inventors and name our aircraft after physical disturbances (*Hurricane*, *Spitfire*, *Tempest*, *Typhoon*) or after cities (the bombers : e.g., *Lancaster* and *Halifax*) or, rather earlier, after national heroes long dead (*Wellington*, *Hampden*) or famous places (*Whitley*, *Blenheim*), although once someone was happily inspired to permit a *Mosquito*, with the differentiating plural *Mosquitos*.

But what of the Army in 1939–45 ? Well, in addition to a mass of jargon (for instance, *category* debased to ineptitude and allowed to father such undesirables as *recategoriz-*

ation), it has coined, or at the least popularized, some very effective slang words and phrases, of which perhaps the most famous is *browned(-)off*, ' fed up ', thoroughly depressed and perhaps rather disgusted. Note that this is not a war-baby ; it has been employed in the Regular Army from certainly not later than 1930 and was in use among R.A.F. personnel in India and at Aden since as early as 1931 or 1932. Yet it was in the years 1939–45 that *browned off* achieved a national currency. Despite its origination in the torrid East, the term derives, not from the sun-browned hills or sun-scorched parade grounds, but from cookery—in short, from those mishaps known jocularly as *burnt sacrifices* (a fertile source of discontent among ' the men-folk of the house '). The approbatory *smashing*, originally Cockney, has been disseminated by the Army, which passed it generously to the R.A.F. (*a smashing job*, a very attractive girl) and to the Navy (*a smashing Jenny* or Wren). The Army also allowed the other Services the use of *stooge*, ' a learner ; a deputy or stand-in ; an over-willing fellow ; a third-rater ' ; *to stooge about*, ' to be on patrol, to cruise about, to delay one's landing ', the verb being almost solely an Air Force usage. The origin is either the American *stool pigeon*, ' informer to the police ; hence, in the theatre, an understudy ', or, as I prefer (the earliest English sense being ' learner '), the ordinary word *student*—via *studious* mispronounced *stoo-djus*. Also originally Army words are these three : *synthetic*, ' artificial ; impractical ' (compare the 1914–18 *ersatz*) ; *snoop around* or *about*, ' to pry ' ; *that shook him*, ' disturbed his equanimity, impaired his complacence '.

From the France of 1940–45 we have already derived *do a Dunkirk*. Other French terms are collaborator (' Ces collaborateurs infâmes ! '), *underground movement* (' le mouvement souterrain '—sometimes shortened to ' le souterrain,' as, in English, we sometimes use the shorter *underground*)*, and *Maquis*, ' Les Maquis ' being those French guerilla fighters who opposed the Nazis in rural France, especially in the scrublands of the Central, and the Southern, East of France. In France *maquis* is ' rough scrub, tough scrub ', adopted from *maquis* (or *makis*), ' wild bushy land in Corsica ', the original being Italian *macchie*, the plural of *macchia*, itself from Latin *macula*, ' a spot, a mesh '.

The Soviet Union has contributed three terms, one directly as in ' the *scorched earth* policy ' of which we heard so much in the three months following Hitler's unannounced invasion of Russia on June 22, 1941, and two indirectly—by allusion to V. M. Molotov, who, born in 1890, became in 1939 the head of the Commissariat for Foreign Affairs and in May 1941 Foreign Commissar. These two are the *Molotov bread-basket*, a rack that, released from an aircraft, rotates as it falls, and scatters, one by one, its load of dozens of incendiary bombs, thus tending to produce a group-conflagration, and the *Molotov cocktail*, a bottle filled with an inflammable mixture (chiefly petrol) and fitted with a wick, or a saturated piece or rag-tape, ignited immediately before it is thrown at, e.g., a tank. *Molotov cocktail* may be the translation of a term coined by the Finns during the Russo-Finnish war.

The war with Japan (early December 1941—August 1945) has revived the popularity of *hara-kiri*—incorrectly *hari-kari*—' suicide by disembowelment ' (from *hara*, ' belly ', and *kiri*, ' to cut '), practised only by other ranks and the ignobles, for nobles and officers do it ceremonially and most ceremoniously, and they call it *seppuku*. In

---

* In, e.g., Paul Brickhill & Conrad Norton's exceptional book, *Escape to Danger*, 1946—the best of the 1939–45 escape books.

1914–18, when the Japanese were with us, we heard little ; in 1941–45 when they were against us we heard much ; of *bushido*, ' code of honour ', strictly, *Bushido*, ' the Samurai code of honour '. Literally *bu-shi-do*, ' military-knight ways '—hence, the customs, ' the book of words ', of the well-born soldier, the term is something of a fake, more or less invented, a few years before the Russo-Japanese war (1904–05), for the use of gullible foreigners. It is the one important Japanese contribution to Western thought in the 1940's.

The American soldiers and sailors did not ' fall ' for it. But they did make two interesting additions to the language : *G.I.* (their equivalent of *Tommy*), ' an ordinary soldier ', from the abbreviation *G.I.*, ' general issue ', as applied to clothes and equipment ; and *jeep*, that extraordinarily useful and versatile cross-country vehicle which came on lease-lend to Britain long before we welcomed the G.I.'s and which has likewise been formed from initials, in this instance *G.P.*, ' (for) general purposes ', hence an adjective, ' general-purpose ', the original form being ' *a G.P. vehicle* '.

Oddly enough, the ' jeep ' (official since 1943) had a precursor in the not dissimilar, ugly but efficient British utility motor-van that in 1939–43 the Army called a *doodlebug*, so named both from the *doodles* one absentmindedly draws on pad or paper and from the resemblance this vehicle bears to a large *bug* or beetle. And so the *doodlebug*, as the V.1 or German *flying bomb* of the latter half of 1944 was called by the general population, Service and non-Service, of Britain at the time, was not, as I have seen it glamorously stated, a spontaneous, genius-attaining creation by civilians but a sense-adaptation, probably made by soldiers or airmen in South-Eastern England, of the earlier, the Army term, by way of the idea, ' a doodlebug, or a jeep, in the air '.

Objects even more unpleasant than the doodlebug were to travel the skyways. Late in 1944 and early in 1945, the same area of England was visited by numbers of projectiles known as V.2 or the *rocket-bomb*, which received no happy nickname but, much as Hitler was usually mentioned as *that man* (cleverly misappropriated by Tommy Handley), was usually referred to as *that bloody nuisance*.

Apparently the Japanese found the *atom bomb* to be something more than a nuisance. The term *atom bomb* is a shortening of the perhaps more sensible, more aptly descriptive *atomic bomb*, which, by the way, was, as a potential, being freely discussed by the Americans before they became involved in the war, as you may see for yourselves if you turn to *The Reader's* (not *The English*) *Digest* of 1941. That the word, like the thing, has come to stay, seems all too probable.

The war has ended, but war responsibilities are with us. In occupied enemy countries our troops were, at first, forbidden and later allowed to *fraternize*, which has therefore modified its meaning from ' to live, to act, as brothers with—or towards—others of one's own race ' to ' doing this with members of an enemy or ex-enemy race ; especially to become friendly with an enemy of the opposite sex '. The slang shape of the word is ' to *frat* ', and he or she who ' frats ' is a *fratter* and the practice is *fratting*.

Which reminds me that the war of 1939–45 has popularized the hitherto official or pedantic *national*, ' one who belongs to a nation ', as in ' a British national —enemy nationals '. Originating, at the beginning of the present century, as a term in the theory of International Law, it has its justification in the fact that it is so very convenient, for it covers sovereign (or president) and subject, citizen and non-citizen.

Nobody can *blue-print* a living language; nobody can furnish an adequate *blue-print* of even the neologisms: such fatuities are best left to bull-dozing bureaucrats and doctrinaire departmentalists. John P. Marquand has, in *So Little Time*, 1943, said, ' He was suddenly tired of all the new words—" streamlined ", " blitz ", " three-point program ", " blueprint " '.

*   *   *

Having considered the preceding terms (a representative, not an exhaustive list), the reader may well ask, ' But where can I find these words? Further, what sources *are* there, in general, for neologisms? Is it all a matter of luck, good or bad, whether I'm kept aware of the new terms creeping—or storming—into the language? '

First, it is nobody's business (except that of the individual himself) to keep him aware of these newcomers. But here are a few hints, several of which are somewhat obvious; my experience, however, is that except among ' the experts ', the extent to which the obvious escapes notice is ' just nobody's business '.

The sources may be divided into two main groups: the current; the lexicographical.

By the current, I mean both the books that are appearing every day, and certain periodicals. It is impossible to say anything useful about the former, although certain writers yield far more than others. Of American novelists, Sinclair Lewis and John P. Marquand are to be signalized; of British, Charles Morgan, Stanley Houghton, Rose Macaulay. One can be more definite about newspapers and other periodicals. The richest American sources that are also trustworthy are *The American Mercury*, *Harper's Magazine*, *The Atlantic Monthly*, *The New Yorker*—and *The* (New York) *Times*. Then there is a periodical that bridges the gap between the academic and the non-academic worlds : *American Speech* takes into account every manifestation of the language as it is spoken and written in the United States, from cant (the language of the under-world) to the classics, from the speech of the commuter to that of the cinema, from the worst of tabloid journalism to the best American writing. We have in Great Britain—in the entire Commonwealth of Nations, indeed—nothing that can be compared with it. To *The American Mercury* our nearest parallel is *John o' London's Weekly*, the most valuable of all British periodical sources. Of British news-papers, the most useful for our purpose are *The Times*, *The Manchester Guardian*, *The Daily Telegraph* ; for journal-ists, there is the Journal of the Institute of Journalists. In South Africa : *The Cape Times*, *The Cape Argus*, *The Johannesburg Star*. For Australia : *The Sydney Bulletin*.

Midway between the current and the lexicographical stands that alert commentary, which takes the form of book or tract. Here again, the United States of America possess something to which we in Britain can offer no rival, no counterpart—the successive carefully revised and considerably augmented editions of H. L. Mencken's *The American Language*, first published in 1918 ; second edition in 1922 ; third in (?) 1928 ; fourth in 1936 ; and the new, ' positively monumental ' one in 1947–48. On the other hand, we have in England something for which, in America, they have to go to both Mencken and *American Speech* and even then do not find some of the ' features ' of the Society for Pure English tracts, which, in addition to dealing with specific themes (the Subjunctive, the Fused Participle, and what-have-you), return at intervals to certain matters of ever-recurring interest, such as neologisms, the most suitable and sensible English forms and plurals of words imported from other languages, and so forth. These tracts constitute a storehouse of information too often ignored by scholars and almost entirely ignored by those who, without pretension to scholarship, yet have some claim to be called educated or even cultured. If you consult the S.P.E. tracts and regularly read *John o' London's Weekly*, and the newspapers mentioned above, you will, within a reasonable interval, find almost every neologism, —with this proviso, that for technicalities you must go to the technical and scientific periodicals.

The lexicographical sources are the more important, perhaps only because they are more convenient; here you find immediately, without having to hunt for it, the word you want. Or maybe you don't. Neologisms fall into two classes : new words or phrases (or new senses of these words and phrases) ; and new usages, in so far as they can be differentiated from new senses. For the United States, the best work on current usage is Perrin's *Index to English*, although H. W. Horwill's *A Dictionary of Modern American Usage* is very useful to the British public ; for Britain, the matchless H. W. Fowler's *A Dictionary of Modern English Usage*, although, since 'Fowler' has not been 'modernized' since its appearance in 1926, my own *Usage and Abusage* (published in April, 1947), is not unuseful, the more so as it contains a section—quite independent of, though necessarily overlapping, this article—on War neologisms and a long section on Vogue Words prevalent since 1918, as well as many entries that simply could not have been made in 1926.

The lexicography of neologisms has always presented a difficulty, not only to the searching public, which, after all, has only to look for them, but also to the lexicographer. Some neologisms are so short-lived, so little used even during their ephemeral life, that they are hardly worthy of record : and it is impossible for the lexicographer to know, although if he possess a genuine flair he may guess, which neologism will live and thrive and which will rapidly fade and die. Moreover, the lexicographer has no infallible means of prophesying whether a slang neologism will achieve acceptance, first by colloquialism, then by familiar English, and finally (if ever) by literary English. Arbitrarily perhaps, yet conveniently, lexicography may be divided into that of Standard or good English and that of slang and other unconventional English.

' First things first ' : Standard before slang. It is advisable to consult the latest supplement to that great work, *The Oxford English Dictionary* ; that to the *Shorter Oxford English Dictionary* ; and that to *The Concise Oxford English Dictionary* in late 1944. Even the supplements to ' The Pocket Oxford ' and ' The Little Oxford ' contain astonishingly up-to-date neologisms. The editors of *Chambers's English Dictionary* have likewise been scrupulously conscientious in the modernization of the only serious rival to ' The Concise Oxford '.

In the United States, *Webster's New International Dictionary* contains, in the most recent recension (late 1944), a quite invaluable supplement* : this constitutes† much the fullest list of post-1939 neologisms, whether in English or American words and whether published in America

---

* ' Supplement ' is perhaps a misnomer, for the list precedes the dictionary proper.

† At the time of writing : mid-August, 1946.

or Great Britain. Nevertheless, one other American dictionary must, even in so cursory an ' aid ' as this, be mentioned as conscientious about, and valuable for its recordings of, neologisms, and that is ' Funk & Wagnalls' or, less familiarly, *The Standard Dictionary*, whether as *The Comprehensive Standard Dictionary* or as *The New Standard Dictionary*, published by Funk & Wagnalls and edited, from about 1910 until his death in 1938, by the erudite and courageous Frank Vizetelly. Politically important, for America as well as for Britain, is the latest edition (*whenever* that may be) of Walter Theimer's *The Penguin Political Dictionary*.

Slang and other unconventional English, both British English and American English, is even more difficult to catch on the wing, cage, and set edibly before the public. American slang has been admirably organized in *The American Thesaurus of Slang*, 1942 (English edition, 1943), by Lester V. Berrey & Melvin Van den Bark ; arranged on the plan of *Roget's Thesaurus*. It contains much that, to us in Britain, will seem not merely new but impossible. Recent English slang terms will swell the third edition of my *A Dictionary of Slang and Unconventional English*, on which I have been working ; but this, like my recently completed *A Dictionary of the Underworld* (British and American), will hardly appear, at the earliest, before late 1948. In the meantime, therefore, you had better, for Service slang of the War years, consult J. L. Hunt & A. G. Pringle's *Service Slang* (Faber & Faber), C. H. Ward Jackson's witty *It's a Piece of Cake* (The Sylvan Press), and my own *A Dictionary of R.A.F. Slang* (Michael Joseph). *Service Slang* contains the slang of the Navy as well as that of the Army and the Air Force ; but a much fuller list of recent naval slang words is that in the glossary (not likely to appear until some months after this article does) by Lieutenant Wilfred Granville, R.N.V.R. Military and naval slangs, fortunately, are a little less ' tricky ' than Royal Air Force slang ; even so, it is advisable to possess a Service glossary,* for not all War novelists and memoirists are so obliging as the authors of that exceptionally good book *Escape to Danger*.

(Written in August 1946 ; published in
The Quarterly Review, January 1947.)

* In 1948 there will appear *Forces' Slang : 1939–1945*, edited by myself : Navy—Wilfred Granville ; Army—Frank Roberts ; Air Force—E. P.

Part Two : SLANG

Army Slang with a Shady Past

FROM the time he is called up, until he ' cops a Blighty ' or something more serious, the soldier uses much slang. The more he uses, the better he feels. Most of his slang words and phrases are expressive : and among the hundred-or-so most expressive of all are the forty-odd that come from cant—that is, thieves' slang or, more accurately, the language of the underworld. The majority of these underworld terms have reached the Army, not direct from criminals, beggars, tramps, and their associates (receivers of stolen goods, street-walkers, low tavern-keepers and their like), but via the very poor and the lowly.

It is obvious that in the forty-odd expressions here glanced at, I have included none that are merely rhyming slang or back slang. Both rhyming and back slang originated in the underworld : they were a means to secrecy and safety, as also was the now dead medial slang, sometimes called centre slang. Back and centre slangs are tedious, though there is one interesting survival of the former—*mur*, rum. Among the earliest rhyming-slang terms, therefore certainly used first by criminals, are *apples and pears*, stairs ; *Cain and Abel*, a table ; *Daisy roots*, boots ; *I suppose*, nose ; *lump of lead*, head ; *mince pies*, eyes ; *pen and ink*, a stink ; *plates of meat*, feet (or a street) ; and the delightful *trouble and strife*, a wife, and *God forbids*, ' kids ' (children), though these two may have arisen when rhyming slang had reached the poor, the Army and the Navy.

When the private soldier or *swaddy* enlists or is called up, he is unaware that the term *swaddy* (mostly used by the Navy and the Regular Army) is a pet-form of *swadgill*, an underworld expression, or perhaps of *swad* (with variation *swadkin*), a dialect word for a soldier. He joins a *mob* or a *push* (a battalion, a battery, a military unit) as in the 19th century the recruits to thievery joined a mob or push of pickpockets ; but he wishes to *do his bit*, as the thief certainly did not—for to *do one's bit* or *do a bit* used to be an underworld phrase for ' to serve a prison sentence '.

The soldier has his *chums*, his *pals*, and his *cullies*: *chum* and *cully* arose in the 17th century underworld, the former as a fellow-prisoner, the latter as a man or a companion ; *pal* in the 18th century, for an accomplice, and deriving from Romany—the Gypsy language of England. If he becomes a batman or officer's servant, the officer is his *bloke*, originally an underworld term for a man.

He detests the *Jacks* or military police, without knowing that *Jacks* originated among criminals ; he detests no less the *narks*, those men who curry favour with their superiors by running messages and doing odd jobs for them, the word *nark* retaining something of its first, its criminal sense, ' a police spy (often *copper's nark*) or a common informer ' ; but he speaks respectfully of the *stool pigeon* or Secret Service agent, blissfully ignorant that *stool pigeon* originally meant, as it still means in England as well as its home, America, ' a police spy '.

If he is detected in wrongdoing, he is *rumbled*, precisely as a criminal was ' rumbled ' by the policeman who ' tumbled to ' his crime. He will be *run* or arrested, or he may describe it as being *nabbed* or *nailed* or *pinched* :

four terms that have been promoted from underworld usage. And if he gets detention or imprisonment, he is *lagged* or *limbered*, two more underworld terms, the former a corruption of *legged* or fettered with *leg*-irons, the latter connected with *limbo*, an old word for prison. And when he goes to prison or maybe only a guard-room, he goes, especially if it be to prison, to *chokey* (a solitary-confinement or ' dark ' cell, in cant) ; to *clink*, the *Clink* being the 16th- and 17th-century underworld term for a certain prison in Southwark, perhaps from the clinking of fetters ; the *cooler*, a word from the United States, which have so obligingly exported a multitude of their slang and cant expressions ; or the *jug*, when he says he has been *jugged* and is nowise cheered by the fact that *jug* is short for *stone jug*, cant for a prison, the *Stone Jug* being an early name for Newgate Prison.

His misfortune may have resulted from nothing worse than a *binge* or ' blow-out ' or a *booze* or drinking bout ; the former from cant *bingo*, brandy, and the latter from cant *booze*, liquor. But it may have resulted from ' souveniring ' or pilfering something he thinks he needs (for instance, a stool for a fire) or would like to have as a souvenir. He describes the process of acquisition (' *convey*, the wise it call ') as *boning* or *hot-stuffing* or *knocking off* or *lifting* or *making* or *nailing* or *nicking* or *pinching* or *snaffling* or *winning*, all of which were originally employed by thieves for their less condonable activities.

To *nail* and to *pinch*, you notice, appear also among the terms for ' to arrest ', the reason being that when one steals a thing one *takes* it illicitly and that when one is arrested one is *taken* by the police. To *hot-stuff* a thing also meant to commandeer or requisition it, and to *snaffle* has (or had) in the Royal Air Force the specific sense, to cut off an enemy 'plane in the air. To *win,* dating from the 17th century, is a euphemism, as was *make* (compare the French slang *faire* in the same sense). Both of these words are used by soldiers not only for outright stealing but also for slightly unlawful acquisition or for ' forgetful ' borrowing.

In 1917 an actual report from a conscientious and energetic Company Sergeant-Major to his Commanding Officer ran thus : ' We've made three shovels last night, sir. That brings us up correct.' What the C.O. in the next sector of the line said when *his* Sergeant-Major had to report a shortage of the same number of shovels is not recorded.

The soldier's other occupations include being *crummy* or itchy with louse-bites and then industriously *chatting* or de-lousing himself : a condition and an exercise not un-known to tramps and beggars, a *chat* meaning a louse as early as the 17th century and perhaps deriving from *chattels,* ' movable property ' or, in its old sense, ' live stock ', *cattle* being a cognate (or connected) word. But he enjoys his *scran* or food. *Scran* began as a tramp's or beggar's word for the broken victuals given him by kind-hearted housewives and carried in his *scran-bag,* a term diverted by the military into the sense ' haversack '. On occasion he *whacks out* (or *up*) his food and his cigarettes among his friends, to whom he gives a liberal share or *whack* : both the verb and the noun were, in the 19th century, employed by thieves, especially burglars, for a gang share-out.

The private no less than the officer takes a pride in his *clobber* or clothes, the word originally signifying, among beggars, ' old clothes ' ; it is of Yiddish origin. The private and the corporal and even the dignified sergeant hasten to attend pay parade announced with a joyful shout of ' Coal up ! ' This coal has nothing to do with fuel : it is the less usual spelling of *cole*, ' money ', though *coal* may possibly be the correct form, for money is the *coal* or fuel of life as well as—to employ a cliché—the sinews of war. *Cole* arose in the underworld nearly three hundred years ago. Soldiers appreciate their *kip* (bed, if they are lucky ; hence, sleep) and they *kip* or *kip down* with alacrity and a feeling of relief. The noun, which is much earlier than the verb, has a thoroughly disreputable origin.

Usually *on the square* or honest in his dealings (among criminals *on the square* used to mean the opposite of *on the cross*, and *to be on the cross* was to be engaged in theft, or to be a thief), he thinks it good fun to *try it on* with the *croaker*, i.e. to bamboozle the medical officer. In the underworld of the early 19th century, *try it on* was a polite way of saying ' to live by theft ', whereas *croaker*, ' a doctor ', did not arise until about 1850.

But the soldier has also to *do stag* or sentry-go ; in old cant, a *stag* was a spy or an informer. He takes part in *gaffs* or raids on the enemy trench ; from *gaff*, ' a fair ' (the fun of the fair). In the raid he may carry a club or *kosh*, as criminals have, since about 1850, carried a *kosh* or offensive weapon, which, odd though it may seem, was also termed a ' life-preserver '. He laughs at shells that don't explode, and speaks of them as ' duds ' or *stumers*. *Stumer* is a racecourse-gangsters' term for a horse that is certain not to win ; the opposite of those ' morals ' or ' dead certs ' which are the ruin of punters.

In a big ' push ' or *stoush* (dialect *stashie* or *stushie*, an uproar or a quarrel—probably connected with the under-world *stash*), the soldier may *go west*. In this poetical phrase for ' to die ', the basic idea is that of the sun

151   L

setting in the west, but *go west* received additional point when, in the 16th to 18th centuries, it was employed by criminals on their journey from Newgate Prison, up Holborn Hill, and on to Tyburn Tree in the west of London : Tyburn gallows, used from the late 12th century until 1783, stood where the present Bayswater and Edgware Roads join with Oxford Street. Greene, in his *Cony-Catching* (the trickeries of which coneys or rabbits, i.e. dupes, were made the victims by swindlers), 1592, says, ' So long the foists [thieves] put their villanie in practise, that West-ward they goe, and there solemnly make a rehearsall sermon at tiborne ', and in 1785 Captain Francis Grose refers the phrase *to ride backwards up Holborn Hill* to the custom whereby criminals due to be hanged rode with their face to the tail of the tumbril. The idea of the American pioneers travelling into the dangerous West may have contributed to the force and the beauty of *to go west.* And in the 20th century we have seen and shall see some of our friends, our acquaintances, our countrymen go to their deaths like a gallant sun dipping over the western horizon, bathed in its glory, in order that a better day may be born : westering to the dark that light may come.

(Reprinted from *John o' London's Weekly*, October 20, 1939.)

In Mess and Field

THE JARGON AND SLANG OF ARMY OFFICERS

THE language of officers in the Army is, in general, the language of the middle class from which most of them come. The once well known ' Army type ' is much less conspicuous than it used to be, and although it still dominates, it now dominates only in staff work and in other technicalities ; it is no longer predominant, and —below a Corps headquarters, at any rate—it hardly sets the prevalent tone of an officers' mess, although it does much to modify it.

There is now far less Indian Army talk than formerly : Poona and Quetta, the Hills and the Plains, the British Raj and the Monsoon, are no longer the staple of conversation. Hindustani words have lost their imperial status and, instead of being assiduously learnt and constantly employed, they tend, except among officers with Indian service, to be smilingly ignored or openly derided. Only two such words are now at all commonly used : *chit* and *wallah* : and even of these two, the latter is fast losing ground. Both have been current for something like a century. *Chit* is still the usual term for almost any bill, account, note, permit, authorization, or brief memorandum. *Wallah* is employed either as ' chap ', ' fellow ', or as ' specialist ' ; for instance, a Catering Adviser is ' the Catering wallah ', a Camouflage Officer is ' the Camouflage wallah '. Nowadays, however, they are also ' the Catering bloke (or merchant) ' and ' the Camouflage merchant (or bloke) '. *Chit* is almost jargon ; *wallah* is entirely slang.

Jargon and slang form the two classes of words—and phrases—by which the speech of officers is most sharply differentiated from that of the ' other ranks' (the N.C.O.'s and men) : the other ranks rarely employ jargon, i.e. technical terms, and their slang is very different from that of the officers. Jargon is on the increase in the Army, as it is in the other combatant Services. Where, of course, there is no ' plain English ' synonym for a technicality, that technicality is not, strictly speaking, jargon, which properly consists in the use of another—and usually it is a longer—word for a simple, generally understood word. Jargon is preferable to ignorance and confusion, but familiarity with technical terms too often and too easily leads to their far too glib use.

Here are several examples of jargon. Instead of such simplicities as ' go ' or ' travel ', *proceed* is used : instead of ' Private John Smith will go on leave or to hospital ' we have ' Private John Smith will proceed on leave . . .', which sounds so very much more important. A ' class ' becomes a *category*, especially in such an order as ' The officers of this unit will appear before the Medical Officer on Tuesday, with a view to a revision of their medical category ', though the latter part of the sentence may be jargonized to ' with a view to recategorization ', which awe-inspiring process may lead to *inhospitalization* or transference to, or entry into, or reception into hospital. Of *recategorization* and *inhospitalization*, the tonic Sir Alan Herbert would, I think, exclaim ' What a Word ! ' He would probably criticize only a shade less stringently the italicized words in the following sentence : ' All reports from units will be *consolidated* in the report drawn up by the

Division ; the Divisional reports will be forwarded to Corps, where they will undergo *consolidation* before being submitted to Command, which will in turn consolidate the reports from the several Corps. The final consolidation will be made by the appropriate Department of the War Office.' To *consolidate* is either to summarize (or abstract) or to incorporate.

Rather different is ' to *liaise* ', for this verb was at first frowned on by the pundits : its usefulness, its convenience —as always happens in the development of a civilized language—soon came to outweigh its objectionableness. It is, in a way, telegraphese for ' to establish liaison with ' and ' to work in liaison with ', which means little (anything ?) more than ' to meet, or get to know ' and ' to co-operate with '. Here is a discreet adaptation of an actual instruction issued from a Corps headquarters :—
' It is necessary for the Chemical Warfare Officer to arrange that Artillery units liaise with local Infantry units in order that the visiting experts from the War Office should have audiences worthy of the military rank and the technical standing of the visitors.'

Liaise began as slang. ' To *make one's number* ' is still slang ; it may be used absolutely, as in ' As soon as I join my unit I must make my number at Brigade ', or in reference to a person, as in ' I must lose no time in making my number with one of the Staff Officers at Division '— in short, to *contact* him. (' To *contact* ' is short for ' to establish contact with ', was originally American, and is now in common use in England ; it is unfortunately displacing ' to meet ' or ' get to know '.) By the way, one ' makes one's number ' with one's *opposite number*, a phrase taken over from civil life. Actually the *opposite number* is the corresponding number : the *opposite number* to a

Brigade Intelligence Officer, for instance, is the Battalion Intelligence Officer on the one hand, the Divisional Intelligence Officer on the other.

Having made one's number with one's opposite number (or numbers), one ' continues the good work ' by *laying on* this or that activity. Army officers never arrange or appoint anything ; they ' lay it on '. As *making one's number* presumably comes from telephony, so *laying on* would seem to derive from the noble trade of plumbing. The people that can safely ' lay on ' almost anything are *topsides*, those who are at the head of a department, of a specialist corps, or of an arm (for instance, the Royal Engineers) of the Service. ' Topside will turn it down cold ' you often hear it said of a valuable but unorthodox proposition.

It is from *topsides* that the choicest reprimands come ! An ordinary reprimand is a *raspberry*, often referred to by other ranks as a *rarzer*, which has been adopted from that form of civilian disapproval which one hears in the gallery of a theatre. ' There'll be a bunch of raspberries issued over that flop at the last exercise ' (the new Army word for manoeuvres), I once heard a much-harassed Staff Officer say with a mournful shake of the head. A severe reprimand is a *rocket*, which blows the victim (who, inevitably, has *blotted his copy-book*) sky high, and an especially severe one is either an *imperial rocket* or an *outsize in rockets*. In the Mess, disapproval or disgust is conveyed by ' I take a poor view—*or* a very poor view —of that ' !) Praise, which is rare, very seldom exceeds the effusiveness of ' Nice work, Jones ! ' : normally, however hard or however well one may work, one is merely *carrying on* or ' doing one's duty ' ; if you exceed your duty and fail, you receive a ' rocket ' (usually imperial), and if you succeed, you receive a mild reproof of the ' It's magnificent, but it's not war ' type.

(Written in May 1942. Published in
The New Statesman, August 1, 1942.)

Words Get Their Wings

THE SLANG OF THE ROYAL AIR FORCE

Corp. A.—*Chiefy* has got on the wrong side of *Groupy*. He expected to go on leave next week. I guess *he's had it*.

Sarge B.—Well, even so, he's more *spawny* than *Flight Louie* Whatshisname, who was all set to begin his leave this morning. Last night, *he went for a Burton*. Fell into *the drink*, they say, after *getting himself tangled in the soup* ; on his way back from the *Crump Dump*— regular *milk-round* if ever there was one !

Corp. A.—Sorry to hear that, 'cause he was a *darned good type*, knew his *gen*, never *shot a line*, and didn't mind being *shot down in flames* himself. But he was *cheesed off* ; probably took a risk.

Sarge B.—Ah, well ! I must *get mobile*. Have to start the *Chain Gang* on something *Squadron Leader Swill* wants done—or was it *The Stationmaster* ?

THAT—with the addition of a few lurid expletives—is the sort of thing you might hear almost any day on an operational station manned by the Royal Air Force. To some it may be almost as unintelligible as a conversation between two dyed-in-the-wool Chicago gangsters would be to a secluded old maid who has never left the most ' Ritzy ' suburb of Boston. But such of the slang terms as are not guessable from their context will be explained hereinafter.

R.A.F. slang is virile and vigorous, graphic and picturesque, irreverent (for the most part) yet not irre-

sponsible, often humorous, occasionally witty ; ' packing
a punch ', yet usually good-natured. Confronted with
death, it tends to become evasive, but faced with peril
it is manly and direct, debonair and insouciant. Youthful,
it is sometimes imitative and sometimes almost truculently
original and independent ; after all, the Royal Flying
Corps (which on April 1, 1918, became the Royal Air
Force) was inaugurated only on May 13, 1912 ; to some
small extent, its slang, like its organization, is still suffering
from the growing-pains inseparable from so rapid an
expansion.

That both the British Army, instituted in the 17th century, and the Royal Navy, instituted in the 16th, should
possess a much larger slang vocabulary than the R.A.F.
is natural enough. Of the three Fighting Services, the
Army has the largest number of words and phrases, yet
the Army has added only a small number to its 1914–18
vocabulary, which, in the main, it still uses. Naval slang,
not quite so extensive, is even more conservative and
traditional than the Army's. The R.A.F., which retains
some of the comparatively few Royal Flying Corps terms
(and these chiefly among the older men and mostly in
slightly different senses), possesses a rapidly increasing
body of words ; in a few years' time, it may have gone
close to rivalling the Navy and the Army in the total
number of slang terms it has in current use.

In peace-time, however, the slang of a Fighting Service
grows much less rapidly and effectively than during a war.
War always produces a rich crop of slang. Both in the
First and in the Second World War it has been very
noticeable that the Fighting Services possess or come to
possess far more new slang terms than civilians acquire.
In support of this statement, the writer may perhaps be

permitted to quote from his recently published book, *A Dictionary of R.A.F. Slang* (with an introductory essay). ' Nor is the reason difficult to ascertain. In the Services, the men live—or should live—a more exciting life ; they deal with new equipment and various weapons ; do things they've never done before—and pretend they never want to do again ; many visit countries strange to them ; many become engaged in a service that is actually instead of nominally active ; all of them mingle in such a companionship as they have never had before they enlisted and will never again have, once they quit the service. Such conditions inevitably lead to a rejuvenation of language—to vividness—to picturesqueness—to vigour ; language becomes youthful, energetic, adventurous. And slang is the easiest way to achieve those ends ; that it is, very often, also the laziest way is irrelevant—nor, if it were relevant, would it much matter, for men speaking vigorously and vividly will not stop at slang. Standard English itself becomes refreshed and enriched.'

That Standard English will enrich itself from the heady springs of Royal Air Force slang, it would be premature to say. Probably, however, it will. From slang, a word ascends to the region of colloquialism, whence it climbs to that of Familiar English, whence, again, it may even mount to that of Literary English. It is not improbable that *You've had it* or (*He's had it*) will be adopted as a proverbial saying, for, from being masonically, hermetically ' Raffish ', it had reached parts of the Army as soon as early 1943 and had gained a certain restricted currency among civilians by the middle of 1944.

The slang of the R.A.F. abounds in telling phrases. Some are general in their scope, a matter of mood or attitude ; one might almost say, an expression of philosophy. Not a very metaphysical philosophy—nothing Berkeleyish, Kantian, Roycean, Bergsonian. But rather, pragmatistic, William-Jamesish. Many are ironical, usually with a self-defensive irony. Many derive from, and some continue to be applied to, operations against the enemy or, at the least, to the true stuff of flying : practical, not theoretical ; not visionary, but experienced. Many, again, are most pertinently allusive to peace-time vocations, these being phrases which receive a sharp, precise twist and a definite tang from that to which they are adoptively applied. Others are very, very rude, and have to be omitted from these respectable pages.

Pride of place must be accorded to *You've had it*, which is ironic, for it means ' You have not had it—and, what's more, you won't get it '—' the article you want, the promotion you seek, the privilege you desire—this, or these, you *cannot* obtain ! ' The writer sadly remembers that while he was at a Recruits Centre, he one day, at tea-time, failed to obtain any jam ; the man that had taken far more than his share remarked, ' You've had it ', to which the deprived party caustically replied, ' No, it seems that *you've* had it.' The origin of the phrase is obscure. Perhaps there is a reference to ' I've had some ' (I know by experience—and don't wish for more) ; probably there is one to the proverbial ' You can't eat your cake and have it '. Most probably, however, the origin lies in the oldish military statement of dolorous fact : ' He has had his issue ', everything that he is entitled to receive, as part of his statutory clothing and equipment, from Stores or Ordnance in short, all those articles with which he could rightfully be issued. A few American airmen have adopted the phrase, which they find arresting and expressive.

He who has definitely 'had it' is, clearly, the man who
has 'fallen in combat' or otherwise fatally. With death
are connected two other phrases very generally used :
gone for a Burton and *no future in it,* which occur mostly in
the forms 'He's gone for a Burton' and 'There's no
future in it'. The former has, in the R.A.F., ousted *gone
west,* which the British Army popularized in 1914–18.
'He is dead' may appear somewhat remote from 'He
has gone for a glass of Burton' : but then, all euphemisms
do, at first, appear remote. It is, however, possible
(though less probable) that the reference may be to
Burtons, the famous tailors, who specialize in ready-made
suits ; in English dialect, 'He's got a wooden suit' means
'He's dead' ; the transition would be 'He's got a
Burton's'. *No future in it* may refer to improfitable or
dead-end work or activities, or it may allude to a foray,
a sweep, a raid that, being dangerous, may preclude the
speaker's future *after* that sortie, in which latter sense it is
evasive—but not cowardly. The former sense recalls the
sometimes jocular, sometimes provocatively ironic query,
Are you happy in (or, *at*) *your work ?,* usually addressed to
a person engaged in a heavy or tedious or uncongenial
task.

Phrases of general application may be exemplified in
What's cooking ?, You're holding up production, Everything (*is*)
under control, and *Hold everything,* of which the first and
the last represent borrowings from the U.S.A., *Hold
everything !* coming from pre-cinematic photography.
What's cooking ? needs no explanation : *You're holding up
production* implies that the person addressed is in the way,
or idle : *Everything's under control* implies a very satisfactory
situation or a successful piece of 'wangling', 'scrounging',
'organization' : and *Hold everything !* means 'Stop what

you're doing, something important has occurred and something more urgent requires to be done'. Also general is *It's a piece of cake*, applied to an easy job or a casualty-free raid.

Indicative of urgency, too, or at the least of expediency, are the sense-linked phrases : *Get cracking !—get weaving ! —get mobile !—get organized !* : of which the last means, ' *Work systematically or more cleverly* ', or ' arrange your affairs more profitably '. The other three are virtually synonymous ; ' Get busy ! ' is what they urge one to do. *Get cracking* has been adopted from the Army, but *Get weaving* is pure ' Raff ', and derived from the weaving or quick dodging tactics of a pilot desirous of avoiding enemy flak or enemy aircraft. *Get some flying-hours in !*, however, is playful for ' have a good sleep ' and *Get some time in !* constitutes a rebuke to a person with only short service.

Nostalgic of civilian life are—to choose only two phrases—*a pair of white gloves* and *play the piano*. The former, referring to the safe return of all bombers or fighter-bombers from a raid, derives from the legal custom whereby, to a judge whose calendar is free of crime, his colleagues present a pair of white gloves. The latter means ' to release bombs, one at a time, from one's aircraft ' : obviously, therefore, an operational phrase.

The operational phrases (operations or aerial offensive become *ops*) are numerous. Here are a few ; several of them have almost lost their original, their truly operational meaning. *To go into a flat spin*, which dates from the First World War, now signifies ' to panic, to become highly excited, to act or talk wildly ' ; *shoot a line*, ' to boast ', derives from a pilot's dropping a stick of bombs in a straight line, and *shoot down in flames* or *shoot down from a great height* signifies no more than to defeat badly in an argument or to refute upon a point of fact. *Tangled in the soup*, 'lost or gone astray in a fog', refers picturesquely to that kind of meteorological inconvenience which is called a 'pea-souper'. *Go through the gate* and *turn up the wick* are slang synonyms for 'to open the throttle full-out in order to fly at maximum speed'. *Frozen on the stick*, 'paralysed with fear', refers to the control-lever or, as it used to be known in 1914–18, 'joy-stick'—from the thrill one obtains from holding it. Both *give her the gun*, 'to accelerate', and *grab for altitude*, 'to become very angry' (originally, and still, 'to try to climb rapidly'), would seem to be of American origin. To *get one's blood back* is to shoot down that enemy aircraft which has 'downed' a near relative or a close friend. Connected with actual operations are *Close hangar doors !* or *Hangar doors closed !*, which not unnaturally means 'Stop talking shop !', and *Pull the chocks away !*, which is a hangar or airfield variation of *Get cracking !* Before an aircraft, prior to making a flight, can taxi along the runway, the wheel-chocks must be pulled away.

Such origins of popular phrases are too objective, some of them almost too technical, to be *Scotch mist*, the R.A.F. term for something imaginary. For instance, a sergeant addressed by a recruit as though he were a mere in-experienced aircrafthand, would probably say 'What'—pointing to his stripes—'do you think these are? Scotch mist?' The joke of it is that Scotch mist is as wetting as most English rain.

But certain single words (and those single words in derivative combinations) are no less interesting, hardly less vivid, than the phrases. With these may be taken such word-groups as *Brains Trust*.

Brains Trust may fairly be included among the R.A.F.

slang terms dealing with ranks and trades, for it is the nickname of the Central Trade Test Board, which examines all Tradesmen (every man in the ranks belongs to some ' trade '-group or other), whether prospective or desirous of promotion ; but it asks questions not answers them. The reference is to the Brains Trust of the British Broadcasting Corporation, which owes the designation to President Roosevelt's even more impressive Brains Trust.

The process of abbreviation will be found to account for numerous terms, but as these are not particularly exciting, the writer will mention only two ; *Wingco* or Wing Commander, and *Swo* or Station Warrant Officer. Rather different is *Groupy*, Group Captain ; and rather different again is *Chiefy*, which represents a Flight Sergeant, and dates from the old Royal Naval Air Service days, when the rank of that man who discharged duties and had privileges similar to those of a Flight Sergeant held the rank of *Chief* Petty Officer. The *Stationmaster*, obviously from the railroads, is that officer who commands an *operational* station or airfield, whereas *Squadron Leader Swill* is the Administrative Officer on any R.A.F. station, one of his duties being the disposal of swill.

Sarge (sergeant) and *Corp* (corporal) have been borrowed from the Army. But whereas the Army speaks of a recruit as a *rooky*, the R.A.F. calls him a *sprog*, which like *erk*, presents an etymological puzzle. By folk-lore rather than by fact, it has been explained in an anecdote to the effect that, in or about the year 1930, a recruit confusing a sprocket with a cog, achieved the unintentional blend, *sprog*, a mistake that immediately achieved popularity and very rapidly spread throughout the R.A.F. It makes a good story, perhaps. Nevertheless, knowing something of the devious ways of slang, the writer prefers that ingenious etymology which derives it from ' frog spawn ', the unpronounceable *rogsp* being back-slanged to *sprog*. Of *erk*, there are four explanations : *erks* (Aircraftmen, Grade II—the ' lowest of the low ') themselves say that their name springs from the *irk*some jobs they so often have to do ; most improbable. Others, notably the members of the Fleet Air Arm, think that it began as ' lower-deck hand ' ; improbable. Yet others believe that this word (used in 1914–18 for an Air Mechanic) sarcastically refers to *erg*, which, in engineering, forms ' the *lowest* unit of work ' ; not improbable. The writer prefers derivation from its original sense, thus :

> *air mechanic*
> *air mech*
> *air mek*
> *airmk*
> *airk*
> *erk,*

which is less fantastic than it may at first appear, for two constants of slang-origin are involved : shortening, and ease of pronunciation ; especially operative in all language-processes is this latter principle.

In the next three terms, no linguistic difficulty presents itself. A *plumber*, to the airmen, is an armourer, and to the officers an Engineering Officer. Humour informs, also, both *the Gestapo* (the R.A.F. Police) and *the Chain Gang*. The latter neatly burlesques the manifold manual tasks performed by the Aircrafthands (General Duties), those handymen of the R.A.F. who attend to anything from garbage to gardening and from coal-heaving to sweeping, the allusion being to those convict-gangs which, to prevent their escape, were chained together while they were engaged in road-making and road-mending.

To the weapons and missiles they use, airmen have given such picturesque names as *chatterbox* for a machine-gun, which pours forth a stream of *confetti* ; a revolver is a *hip-flask* ; *cookie*, American in origin, is either a 4,000-or an 8,000-pound bomb, unpleasant to digest ; and a *torpedo* is a *mouldy*, as, in the Navy, it has been for almost half a century. The Navy appropriated *mouldy* from English dialect, where it means a mole : from under-ground to underwater activity requires only an easy step.

Perhaps more generally interesting, however, is the aircraft group. An aircraft is known as a *kite* or, occasion-ally, a *crate* ; the latter, like the obsolescent—indeed, almost obsolete—*bus*, dates from the old Royal Flying Corps days. All three exhibit that humorous depreciation which characterizes so much of the slang employed by the combatant Services. *Spit*(fire), *Hurry* (Hurricane), and *Cat*(alina) may be said to have been self-generated, almost parthenogenetic : they made themselves. But *Hurrybomber*, for a Hurricane fighter bomber, is not slang ; it is a rather unhappy piece of journalese. Almost as simple are *Annie* for an Anson, often known also as *Limping Annie*, from its uneven engine-note ; *Lizzie* for a Lysander, in reference both to its first three letters (*Lys*) and to (*tin*)*Lizzie*, an old name for a Ford automobile ; *Maggie* for a Magister ; and *Tiffy* for a Typhoon. A *Ham-bone* is a Hampden Bomber, with a vague allusion to its shape. *Wimpey* for a Wellington is clever, for it refers to Mr. J. *Wellington Wimpey*, the esteemed com-panion of Popeye the Sailor in a famous series of comic cartoons.

Of the names for German aircraft the best-known are

M

Mess or *Messer*, a Messerschmitt ; *He, Me and You*,
Heinkel, Messerschmitt and Junkers, from the abbreviations *He, Me, Ju* (pronounced *you*) ; and *the Abbeville
Kids* or Focke-Wulf pursuit planes, which the R.A.F.
encountered first in the skies over Abbeville, *Kids* having
been suggested by the Dead-End Kids of pre-war cine-
matic fame. These young actors were at one time thought
to have landed themselves in a Hollywood dead-end.

From the numerous operational terms, only a few can
be selected. *Footle around* is to circle in one's search for a
target ; this, to adventurous or impatient spirits, being a
waste of time : *futile*, whence it derives. *The deck* is the
land as opposed to *the drink* or sea ; the latter, which is
old nautical slang adopted by Naval airmen, led to the
former, one good name—like one good turn—deserving
another ; *the Drink* is the English Channel, and *the Big
Drink* is the Atlantic Ocean, the latter having been
current among sailors since at least as early as 1890. To
take off, hurriedly, to oppose enemy aircraft is to *scat*,
which, in the same way as American *scram* shortens
' scramble ', shortens ' scatter '. *Party*, an air-battle, ' a
good time being had by all ', reminds the writer that to
go into action (' Yoicks ! ', ' Tally-ho ! ', and all that)
is known as *to go to the movies*, where one has a splendid
view of some truly remarkable pictures. A bombing-
route that one often flies over, especially in the early
morning, is a *milk-round*. One of the most heavily bombed
areas is the Ruhr or *Crump Dump*, which is pitted with
crump-holes or bomb-craters ; *crump* in 1914–18 signified
the explosion of a German 5·9 field-gun, the word being
echoic (*cr-r-rump*). And to bomb, especially to bomb
heavily, is to *prang* a target. This expressive, partly echoic
word would seem to blend *prod* and *bang*.

Information concerning operations—or anything else —is *gen*, perhaps used even more frequently than the frighteningly ubiquitous *He's had it*. Obviously not, as formerly was supposed, from ' genuine ', for why those derivative phrases *pukka gen*, genuine information or trustworthy news—*phoney gen*, doubtful information— *duff gen*, incorrect information ? *Pukka* is Hindustani for ' authentic ', *phoney* comes from the American underworld (which had corrupted it from a word familiar to 18th–19th-century English criminals), and *duff* ' inferior, trashy ', is also an underworld term, not unconnected with ' dough '. The correct explanation of the origin of *gen* is that it represents the rhetorically most important syllable in ' for the *gen*eral information of all ranks ', a phrase sacred to Navy, Army, Air Force.

Such a description as *phoney gen* flows naturally from an intellectual attitude or, at worst, a mood. Attitude or mood, perhaps both mood and attitude, are expressed in *smashing* (excellent) and *ropey* (inferior, bad) ; also in *bind* and in that trio of synonyms *brassed off* and *browned off* and *cheesed off*. To *bind* a person is to bore him, to irritate him : that which ties us, binds us, and that which ties us ends, very often, in becoming a source of exasperation. There may also be an allusion to that irritability which so often results from being *bound* or constipated.

Brassed off, *browned off*, *cheesed off* are synonymous with ' fed-up '—bored and weary and either disgusted or depressed. *Brassed off* has been borrowed from the Navy, where its earliest application was to the emotion or the mood caused by a long turn at polishing the ship's brass-work ; compare the Navy's *to part brass-rags*, to quarrel. *Browned off* is military in origin : it arose in the Regular Army, apparently in India, somewhere about the year

1930. Probably it would be much too fanciful, to attribute it to disgust at the brown, baked hills of India ; perhaps rather too fanciful to relate it to being in a *brown* study ; but fairly safe to trace it to the kitchen where an over-baked dish may be literally *browned off* the private dining-table or the hotel menu, there being a parallel in the old kitchen-deriving slang phrase *done brown* (swindled, circumvented, defeated). Of these three synonyms, the most indigenously ' Raffish ' is *cheesed off*, which may have been prompted by *browned off*, with the necessary transition in the *brown* or *brownish* cheese-rind ; that rind, moreover, is inedible—hard to stomach.

There remains but one thing to add. The inter-influence between the British and American Air Forces is more extensive than the preceding paragraphs might lead the general public to suppose ; the interlocking process, which has already gone far, will increase both in extent and in intimacy.

(Written in January–February, and published in
Chambers's Journal in July–August, 1945.)

Cant

THE LANGUAGE OF THE UNDERWORLD

CANT is the learned word—and a very convenient 'telegraphese'—for the language of the underworld; and by the underworld is meant, not only criminals and their associates—for instance, *fences* or receivers of stolen goods—but also beggars and tramps.

It is misleading to speak of cant as Underworld Slang; it is still more misleading to speak of it as Thieves' Slang: despite the fact that many underworld terms creep into slang, cant is not slang at all.

It is a language. A modified language, in that all the small coin of speech—*a* and *the*, *I* and *you* and *he*, *in* and *at* and *by* and *with*, *and* and *but*, *be* and *have*—is the same in cant as in Standard English. It is only the key words, words vital to the underworld, which are different : but how very different they are ! Only an adept like Godfrey Irwin (though he is more than that) or an initiate like Bill Sykes would know the meanings of the cant words for acquiring, taking, seizing, stealing ; for running away, breaking prison, escaping ; for burgling, swindling, arson, kidnapping, shooting, killing ; for arresting, sentencing, imprisoning, hanging or electrocution ; for informer, policeman, detective, lawyer, judge ; for prison and penitentiary, police station and law-court ; for drugs, jewels, motor-cars, trains ; for doctor and clergyman ; for honest citizen and the various kinds of pervert ; for man, woman, girl, child ; for burglar, petty thief, con-

171

fidence man, professional killer ; for the working and non-working tramp ; for working, eating, entertainment, sleeping ; for lock, window, door, room, house, building (especially a bank) ; for stairs, roof, safe ; for money, gold, silver, clothes, furniture ; for bread and butter, meat and bacon, milk and cheese, and drinks ; for dynamite and glycerin ; for bombs, machine-guns, rifles, revolvers, knives, and the ironically named life-preservers ; for village, town, city, country ; for dogs and horses, sheep and cattle ; etc., etc., etc.

Cant is, in short, a secret language, with only the criminally important words disguised. And in that language, many of the terms live for centuries ; comparatively few terms are discarded before the *flatties*, ordinary policemen, and *busies*, detective police, come to know them. (Cant is far more static and conservative than slang is.) But they do change at last. In a very popular play of the late 1930's, the phrase *cracking a crib*, for burgling a house, was used ; for some forty-two years now, the usual underworld phrase has been *screwing a joint*.

Certain cant words have been adopted into general slang ; a few have become ordinary colloquialisms ; and here and there an underworld term has been promoted to the status of Standard English. Instances of these various ascents are *bloke* and *cove*, *cully* and *chum* and *pal* ; *booze* (both noun and verb) and *grub* ; *bingo*, corrupted in form and sense to *binge*, and *stingo* ; to *doss* and to *snooze* ; to *lope* and to *hike* ; to *bilk* and to *do*, swindle ; a *mug* and a *hick* ; to *nab*, to *nail*, to *snaffle* ; *rum* and *queer*, which, until the 19th century, were direct opposites—*queer* (from German) meaning ' damaged, inferior, cheap, worthless ', whereas *rum* meant ' unimpaired, superior, costly, the best of its kind '. Well, why the change in the sense of *rum* ? Because a rum thief, for example, was the best to members of the underworld, but the worst to the police and the general public.

There is cant in almost every language of Europe, in Asia, in the United States, in Canada, South Africa, Australia, New Zealand. It seems to have flourished (and risen) first in France, probably as early as the 12th century, and is seen at its literary best about 1460, in Villon. In Germany a glossary of cant was published about 1490, and some twenty years later Martin Luther had a hand in *Liber Vagatorum*, a Book of Vagabonds. In the 1530's, at the latest, cant appeared in England. In the 16th century, too, it arose in Italy and Spain. In the United States, somewhere about 1770.

' In America ', says Godfrey Irwin (a great American authority on the subject : who lived for years as a tramp and then turned to the newspaper-reporting of crime), ' the tramp is largely responsible for the spread of this language, and it is practically impossible to say where the more or less law-abiding vagrant and the lawless criminal can be differentiated by their speech. The tramp is passing ; the criminal is on the increase, and he is using the tramp cant of old with greater frequency '—and, it must be added, evolving a language of his own.

Turning to Europe, Irwin remarks that ' in shaping their secret language, the European vagabond and criminal drew on the relatively little known Gypsy [though not until the 16th century] and Hebrew [or, rather, Yiddish] for words and phrases ; recruits from more educated circles brought Greek and Latin terms to the canting crew, and then, as now, new situations and ideas called forth new words and phrases until the whole

173

structure became so mixed-up that it is often difficult to say just where this expression or that really originated. In modern times, words from other lands have been superadded.'

To quote yet further from Godfrey Irwin's *American Tramp and Underworld Slang*, which I had the privilege and pleasure of publishing for him back in 1931 :—' One of the most misunderstood languages of the day, and at the same time one of the most interesting, is that of the underworld, concerning which so much curiosity is shown and of which so little is understood by those who do not move within its exclusive circles. Writers of popular tramp and crime fiction are mainly responsible for what little is known, and at the same time are responsible for many glaring errors in their use of cant.' Among the best-known writers dealing with criminals and tramps are Josiah Flynt, Jack London, G. H. Mullin, Charles Francis Coe, James Burke of the United States ; James Greenwood, Edgar Wallace and the utterly dependable James Curtis of England. (To mention invidiously the names of English writers whose façade is superior to their interior would only involve me in tiresome controversy that might become extremely pertinent on my part and somewhat acrimonious on the part of the indicted authors.)

An excellent example of English cant is to be found in ' The Autobiography of a Thief ', in Horsley's *Jottings from Jail*, ca. 1887, although it is much too long for quotation here ; a good contemporary English author whose works are particularly rich in cant is James Curtis, whose *The Gilt Kid* and later books are thoroughly well worth reading as novels. But I shall quote a tabloid from Don Castle's *Do Your Own Time*, 1938. ' Don Castle ' is an American journalist, who in 1934–35 served a sentence

in the great convict prison of San Quentin on a frivolously
trivial charge. It is a convict's story, taken down verbatim
by ' Don Castle ' :—' Th' joke was on me. Th' beak was
a Hebe, an' th' dicks knew he was wrong ; so they kep'
him on th' spot long enough t' make him promise t' give
the broad a five spot in Walla Walla.

' Y'see, th' skirt was th' cutor's lay, an' t' hand her a
fin like that set pretty tough with him ; so he gets me t'
tommy-gun the tecs. I was in a creep-joint when they
comes in f'r a pay-off on a load of M, an' I let 'em have
it—fas'. They knocked off without a whisper. I scrams,
an' am batting up th' stem at about sixty when a dumb
flat-foot yanks me t' th' kerb. He makes th' bus, an' pipes
th' Tommy, an' a coupla quarts o' alky, so what does
th' nob do but bury me f'r th' night.

' Th' nex' mornin' they try t' hang th' torpedoin' on me,
but th' beak gets th' office, and comes down. He goes f'r
me, puts me on th' bricks, an' hands me two grand an'
tells me t' breeze th' burg ; which I does.

' Well, when I hits Frisco th' bulls know me. They
frisk me an' pipe th' case dough. I tries t' tell them it's
square jack, but they don't fall, an' th' nex' thing I knows
I'm doin' a ten-spot in college.'

Here is the author's ' translation ' :—

' The joke was on me. The judge was a Jew, and the
detective knew he was crooked ; so they forced him
to promise to give the girl five years in Walla Walla
penitentiary.

' You see, the girl was the judge's mistress, and to
sentence her to five years went against his grain ; so he
gets me to kill the detectives with a tommy-gun. I was
in a gambling joint that moved to a different spot each
night, when the detectives came in to get their share of

graft on a shipment of morphine ; and I shot them several times. They died without a whisper. I beat it, and am driving my car up the street at sixty miles an hour when a dumb policeman forces me to the kerb. He searches the car, and finds the tommy-gun, and a couple of quarts of alcohol ; and what does he do but put me in a detention cell all night.

' The next morning the police try to hang the killings on me, and the judge gets notified of what's going on, and comes down to the jail. He arranges an alibi for me, and gets me released, and hands me 2,000 dollars, and tells me to leave town, which I do.

' Well, when I arrive in San Francisco, the police know me, search me, and find the limited amount of money I have. I try to tell them it is honest money, but they won't believe me, and the next thing I know I'm doing ten years in prison.'

(March 1942. Published in
The Nineteenth Century and After, January 1943.)